COOKING FOR TWO

Marguerite Patten

HAMLYN
LONDON · NEW YORK · SYDNEY · TORONTO

The author and publishers wish to thank the
following for their co-operation in supplying
colour photographs for this book

Argentine Beef Bureau	Steak Diane, page 27
	Beef Olives, page 31
Plumrose Ltd.	Bacon Grill with Corn Cakes, page 31
Taunton Cider	Taunton Chicken page 51

Cover picture shows Escalopes of veal
garnished with chopped yolk and white of
hard-boiled eggs (see page 26) served with
asparagus and courgettes.
Photograph by John Lee
Line illustrations by Gay John Galsworthy

Published by
The Hamlyn Publishing Group Limited
London · New York · Sydney · Toronto
Astronaut House, Feltham, Middlesex, England

Printed in England by Cox & Wyman Limited
Fakenham, England
ISBN 0 600 38035 1

Contents

Introduction

At some time or another most of us have to cook for two people; it may be when young and sharing a flat; when newly married; or when a Mother is left with a child during the day so there are just two for a mid-day meal. Even when you have brought up a family, probably the time will come when they all leave home, and once again you find yourself cooking for two.

Let us look at some of the advantages of cooking for two people.

It is fun to have pleasant meals together and you do not have to please lots of varying tastes.

Many interesting foods *are* available in the amounts to serve two, for example you can buy 1 grapefruit, 1 avocado pear, 1 aubergine, 1 green pepper, 2 herrings, 2 trout, 2 chops, 2 joints of chicken, etc.

Modern packaging of foods, like bacon, keep it fresh and refrigerators store 'left-overs' safely, so you can prepare for two dishes or two meals at one time.

By the way, I disagree with the comment that you 'do not need' a home freezer for two alone. If you are investing in a new refrigerator choose one with a good sized freezing compartment. It will save you shopping time, money and effort.

Today the quality and variety of convenience foods – canned, dehydrated and frozen, as well as prepared meats, etc., are so good that you can feed well with little effort. Many of these dishes are too sophisticated for family tastes and too expensive to buy for large numbers, but very suitable for two people alone.

Although it is easier, and certainly more interesting, to shop and cook for two people, rather than one alone, it does present some of the same problems.

It is difficult to buy a sufficiently small quantity of *certain* foods.

It hardly seems worthwhile using lots of saucepans for such small amounts of food.

One is so often left with tiresome little 'bits' of food.

At the stage in life when you 'cook for two', you may both be working, and short of time.

Most people complain of being 'hard-up', but there are many couples who are particularly short of money – when setting up the first home on small salaries or when retired and living on small pensions or incomes.

Yes, these are some of the problems, and in the pages that follow I have tried to indicate some of the answers for you.

I hope you enjoy using this book and that it will help you cook well for two.

Marguerite Patten

Useful facts and figures

Oven Temperatures

The following chart gives the conversions from degrees Fahrenheit to degrees Celsius (formerly known as Centigrade) recommended by the manufacturers of electric cookers.

Description	Electric Setting	Gas Mark
very cool	225°F–110°C	$\frac{1}{4}$
	250°F–130°C	$\frac{1}{2}$
cool	275°F–140°C	1
	300°F–150°C	2
very moderate	325°F–170°C	3
moderate	350°F–180°C	4
moderate *to*	375°F–190°C	5
moderately hot	400°F–200°C	6
hot	425°F–220°C	7
	450°F–230°C	8
very hot	475°F–240°C	9

Note. This table is an approximate guide only. Different makes of cooker vary and if you are in any doubt about the setting, it is as well to refer to the manufacturer's temperature chart.

COMPARISONS OF WEIGHTS AND MEASURES

It is useful to note that 3 teaspoons equal 1 tablespoon; the average English teacup is $\frac{1}{4}$ pint; the average English breakfast cup is $\frac{1}{2}$ pint; and a B.S.I. measuring cup, used in recipes, holds $\frac{1}{2}$ pint or 10 fluid ounces.

It should be noted that the American pint is 16 fluid ounces, as opposed to the British Imperial and Canadian pints which are 20 fluid ounces. The American $\frac{1}{2}$ pint measuring cup is 8 fluid ounces, and is therefore equivalent to $\frac{2}{5}$ British pint. In Australia the British Imperial pint, 20 fluid ounces, is used for liquid measures. Solid ingredients, however, are generally calculated in the American cup measure. In America, standard cup and spoon measurements are used.

METRICATION

For quick and easy reference when buying food, it should be remembered that 1 kilogramme (1000 grammes) equals 2·2 pounds (35$\frac{3}{4}$ ounces)–i.e. as a rough guide, $\frac{1}{2}$ kilogramme is about 1 pound. In liquid measurements 1 litre (10 decilitres or 1000 millilitres) equals almost exactly 1$\frac{3}{4}$ pints (1·76), so $\frac{1}{2}$ litre is $\frac{7}{8}$ pint. As a rough guide, therefore, one can assume that the equivalent of 1 pint is a generous $\frac{1}{2}$ litre. Where an accurate conversion is necessary only decilitres are given. Where less important the rounded litre figure is also included.

A simple method of converting recipe quantities is to use round figures instead of an exact conversion, taking 25 grammes to 1 ounce, and a generous $\frac{1}{2}$ litre to 1 pint. Since 1 ounce is exactly 28·35 grammes and 1 pint is 568 millilitres, it can be seen that these equivalents will give a slightly smaller finished dish, but the proportion of liquids to solids will remain the same and a satisfactory result will be produced.
1 dl. (decilitre) = 100 ml. (millilitres).

A PRACTICAL APPROACH

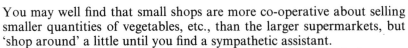

On this, and the next page, you will find suggestions for dealing with some of the problems outlined on page 4.

Buying Small Quantities

You may well find that small shops are more co-operative about selling smaller quantities of vegetables, etc., than the larger supermarkets, but 'shop around' a little until you find a sympathetic assistant.

At the same time remember that you can store many foods for some days in the refrigerator or a cool larder. Vegetables keep well in racks with plenty of air circulation around them.

Often one large can or packet of food is cheaper than two small ones. Stop before buying though and decide *IF* you will be able to use all the contents, for it is not economical if you waste some. I have made a special feature in this book of giving recipes that use half a can of fruit, etc., so you have two entirely different dishes from one basic food.

Plan ahead so you do not become 'panicked' into buying something expensive because you cannot think of what to cook. On the other hand, do not become so rigid in your planning that you cannot take advantage of foods in season when they are exceptionally good and inexpensive.

Use your cooker wisely, for fuel costs money. If you are using the oven fill it up. You can cook vegetables in foil or covered containers (see under Avoiding Excess Washing-Up) instead of in saucepans. You can cook or heat soup in the oven, and you can cook fruit or jacket potatoes to use for another meal.

Most of the main sections in this book have Budget recipes, see pages 14–15, 21–24 and 38–39.

Saving Time

Shop for several days if possible and store the foods carefully.

Prepare two meals at one time or some of the ingredients for a second meal, e.g. if you need chopped onions in a dish for Monday *and* for Tuesday, why not chop them together and wrap half in foil or put it into a tightly sealed polythene container?

If you are cooking jacket potatoes for today why not cook extra ones? Skin these while warm and they are ready to slice for sauté potatoes or to mash for another day.

If you are cooking fruit, prepare a little extra to flavour a fruit trifle.

If you consistently think ahead you will save a great deal of time.

Make sensible use of dehydrated vegetables, frozen ready-coated fish, canned sauces, soups, etc.

Invest in a pressure cooker for speedy cooking of stews, etc. A typical stew can be cooked in 15 minutes at 15 lb. pressure.

Avoiding Excess Washing-Up

If you like a variety of different vegetables for a meal there is no need to use separate saucepans for each variety, you can either:

a) put each kind of vegetable in foil, season lightly and gather the foil into a little 'bundle'. Lower the 'parcels' into boiling water, obviously adding the vegetables that need the shortest cooking time later. You can use the 'parcel' idea when poaching fish, etc.

b) put some vegetables, potatoes, carrots, etc., into the boiling salted water, then, later, add 'parcels' of peas, beans, etc.

c) use vegetable 'baskets'. These are generally sold with pressure cookers but they can be put into large saucepans.

d) you can cook vegetables in salted water in covered containers in the oven. Use attractive ovenware that can be used for serving dishes too; strain the vegetables, then replace in the dish. It is now possible to buy very elegant heatproof dishes that are used as saucepans but also are suitable as serving dishes.

Using Left-Overs

When you buy, prepare and cook food just for two people, you are bound on occasions to get some left. Here are suggestions for using these:

Meat: everyone likes to buy a joint of meat sometimes; page 33 gives a list of ways to use any left.

If you have any stews or casseroles left, give these a change of flavour by adding curry paste, soy sauce, chopped herbs or topping them with pastry or a cobbler mixture (see page 41).

Fish: this is a very perishable food, so use left-overs carefully. You can make Crunchy fish pie, page 25, Fish cream, page 21, or blend the fish with an interesting mayonnaise for a salad. Left-over fish makes an excellent filling for an omelette (see page 53).

Cheese: people who enjoy cheese will want an interesting cheese tray at the end of a meal. This means buying a variety of different cheeses, some of which are unsuitable for cooking. Use these as toppings for salads blended with mayonnaise, or use as sandwich or omelette fillings.

Pastry: whether you buy or make pastry you will often have pieces left over. Roll these out, line small patty cases and bake 'blind'. Store in an airtight tin or freeze these. You can then use them for filling with fruit, jam or savoury ingredients such as fish, blended with mayonnaise, chopped ham, mixed with scrambled egg, etc.

Chicken: you may become tired of buying chicken portions and want a 'real' roasting chicken, in which case you will have a lot left over. Page 47 gives some suggestions to use cooked chicken.

Sauces: it really is very troublesome to make a very small amount of a sauce, so cook enough for 2 meals. Cover the sauce left with damp greaseproof paper. Reheat, whisking briskly.

Bread: keep bread, well wrapped of course, in the refrigerator. It keeps fresh for a very long time. Or freeze sliced bread, and help yourself to slices as required; they toast or fry perfectly when frozen.

How Will I Manage When I Entertain?

After cooking for two people only, it will seem a rather major effort to prepare a meal for 4, 6 or even more people. I have not given a special section on entertaining in this book, for I would consider many of the recipes sufficiently interesting for your guests. Simply increase the quantities in proportion to cater for the number of people expected, and have the kind of menu where quite a lot of the preparation can be done beforehand.

MEAL STARTERS AND SNACKS

Many dishes that are served as a meal starter would be equally suitable for a light snack too.

You can serve the following as meal starters

Avocado pears–served in various ways. Check that the pears are just ripe (i.e. they yield to a gentle touch) if you wish to serve them within 24 hours. Ripen as suggested opposite.

Grapefruit–canned or fresh. This can be served chilled with sugar, or warmed with a little sugar and butter and spice. *Grapefruit Cocktails* are made by blending canned or fresh grapefruit segments with other fruits in season, or with diced cheese or prawns or shrimps. These savoury mixtures should be served on shredded lettuce.

Fruit juices–orange, pineapple, etc., make good meal starters.

Vegetables, such as asparagus, artichokes or salads make excellent meal starters, or a more sustaining snack if you use protein in the salad.

Fruits

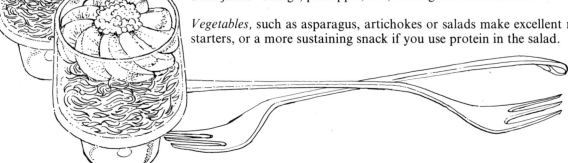

Cauliflower Vinaigrette

Cooking time: 3 minutes
Serves: 2
To store: for up to 12 hours in the refrigerator.

MENU
Cauliflower Vinaigrette
Moussaka (*page 35*)
Apple Ginger Creams (*page 67*)

Do *not freeze* completed dish. (Frozen cauliflower can be used– cook for 2 minutes only.)

IMPERIAL	METRIC	AMERICAN
½ medium *or* 1 small cauliflower	½ medium *or* 1 small cauliflower	½ medium *or* 1 small cauliflower
seasoning	seasoning	seasoning
1 garlic clove	1 garlic clove	1 garlic clove
½ teaspoon made-mustard	½ teaspoon made-mustard	½ teaspoon made-mustard
pinch sugar	pinch sugar	pinch sugar
2 tablespoons olive oil	2 tablespoons olive oil	2–3 tablespoons olive oil
1 tablespoon white wine vinegar *or* lemon juice	1 tablespoon white wine vinegar *or* lemon juice	1 tablespoon white wine vinegar *or* lemon juice
1 large carrot	1 large carrot	1 large carrot
1 firm large tomato	1 firm large tomato	1 firm large tomato
1 teaspoon capers	1 teaspoon capers	1 teaspoon capers

Divide the cauliflower into neat pieces. Cook for 3 minutes in well seasoned water. Drain. Meanwhile, crush the garlic, mix with the mustard, sugar, a little seasoning, oil, vinegar or lemon juice. Add the grated carrot. Spoon over the cauliflower. Allow the cauliflower to become cold then put on to individual plates and garnish with tomato slices and capers.

Avocado Pears

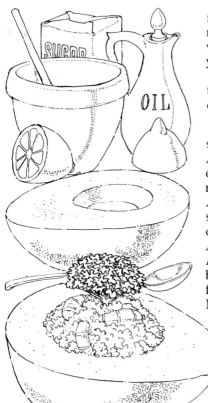

This fruit is a most versatile one. It can be made into a delicious soup (see page 13), and it can be used as a sustaining ingredient in many salads.

The flesh discolours very quickly and easily, so always sprinkle with lemon juice, or an oil and vinegar or lemon juice dressing, when slicing the fruit.

To save shopping time and money, buy several pears when they are reasonable. If you store them in a cool place they will take some days to ripen. If you put them into the airing cupboard they will ripen within a very short time. Gentle pressure will tell you when they are ripe, they should yield to the touch.

Avocado pears are rich in protein, so are an excellent course in a meal that has little meat, etc. One large pear is enough for two as a meal starter or for one as a light meal.

SOME QUICK WAYS TO SERVE AVOCADO PEARS

Avocado Vinaigrette: make a dressing with approximately 2 tablespoons oil, seasoning, pinch sugar and 1 tablespoon lemon juice. Halve the pear, remove the stone and fill with the dressing.

Avocado with Shellfish: prepare the avocado as above and fill the centre with shellfish in mayonnaise; this can be flavoured with a little tomato purée, or ketchup or curry powder.

Avocado de Luxe: fill with shellfish as above and pieces of smoked salmon.

Baked Avocado Pears: fill the halved pears with cream cheese, or fish blended with a little left-over white sauce. Top with breadcrumbs, bake for 20 minutes in a very moderate oven, 325–350°F (170–180°C), Gas Mark 3–4.

Avocado Cream

No cooking
Serves: 2
To store: cover (exposure to the air darkens the avocado pear) and keep in a cool place for several hours only.

MENU
Avocado Cream
Curried Eggs (*page 52*)
Fruit Salad and Ice Cream

To freeze: see above.

IMPERIAL	METRIC	AMERICAN
1 large ripe avocado pear	1 large ripe avocado pear	1 large ripe avocado pear
1 tablespoon oil	1 tablespoon oil	1 tablespoon oil
1 tablespoon lemon juice	1 tablespoon lemon juice	1 tablespoon lemon juice
seasoning	seasoning	seasoning
5 fl. oz. ($\frac{1}{4}$ pint) soured cream	125 g. ($\frac{1}{8}$ litre–1$\frac{1}{2}$ dl.) soured cream	5 fl. oz. ($\frac{2}{3}$ cup) soured cream
few drops Tabasco sauce	few drops Tabasco sauce	few drops Tabasco sauce
lettuce	lettuce	lettuce

Halve the avocado pear, remove the pulp from the skin. Mash this with the oil and lemon juice, then add the seasoning, soured cream and Tabasco sauce. Serve on a bed of shredded lettuce.

To vary

This mixture can be made more sustaining for a light snack if about 4 oz. (100 g.) cottage or cream cheese is blended with the avocado mixture. Or serve fingers of cheese with an *Avocado and Prawn Cocktail:* this would either make a snack or enable you to make 1 avocado pear serve 4. Prepare mixture as above. Spoon on to shredded lettuce, top with prawns (or other shellfish) tossed in a little mayonnaise.

Pâtés to make

To store: in a refrigerator for 2–3 days, covered with foil or melted butter.

To freeze: cover well and use within 4–6 weeks.

There are many ingredients from which to produce a pâté. The quantities given below would serve 5–6 as an hors d'oeuvre or 2–3 people with salad, etc., as a sustaining snack.

Aubergine Pâté: buy 2 medium sized aubergines (eggplants). Wash, dry, do not peel. Halve lengthways and brush the cut side with plenty of olive oil. Cook in a slow oven until very dark brown in colour. Mash the aubergine pulp with seasoning, lemon juice, 1–2 cloves crushed garlic and a little more olive oil.

Fish Pâtés: choose smoked salmon (buy pieces if possible–these would be slightly cheaper than slices), smoked trout, cooked kippers, bloaters or smoked haddock. Mince or chop the fish very finely. To each 4 oz. (100 g.) fish allow 2 oz. (50 g.–$\frac{1}{4}$ cup) butter, 1 crushed garlic clove, 3–4 tablespoons thick cream, the juice of $\frac{1}{2}$ lemon, shake of pepper. Beat all the ingredients together or blend in a liquidiser.

Meat Pâtés:
1) Use the recipe above but choose *lightly* fried chickens' livers or calf's liver instead of fish (fry in plenty of butter).
2) *Liver and Tongue Pâté:* this is a more elaborate pâté and it would therefore be wiser to make enough to serve up to 8 people as an hors d'oeuvre, or 4 people as a snack. Fry 1 chopped onion in 3 oz. (75 g.–$\frac{3}{8}$ cup) butter until soft. Add 8 oz. (200 g.) diced liver and cook for a few minutes, then chop very finely. Tip the onion, liver and any butter left into a basin, add 6 oz. (150 g.) finely chopped cooked tongue, 2 chopped gherkins, seasoning and 1–1$\frac{1}{2}$ tablespoons sherry. Beat all the ingredients together or blend in a liquidiser. Press into a dish. Allow to cool.

Pâté Stuffed Eggs

Cooking time: 10 minutes
Serves: 2. Use as an hors d'oeuvre.
To store: in a cool place for limited period only.

MENU
Pâté Stuffed Eggs
Trout in Lemon Cream Sauce (*page 20*) with Green Salad and Jacket Potatoes
Fresh Fruit

Do *not freeze* eggs.
Pâté *freezes* well.

IMPERIAL	METRIC	AMERICAN
2 eggs	2 eggs	2 eggs
1 oz. pâté (half small can)	25 g. pâté (half small can)	1 oz. pâté (half small can)
several lettuce leaves	several lettuce leaves	several lettuce leaves
1 tomato	1 tomato	1 tomato
2 gherkins	2 gherkins	2 gherkins
2 tablespoons mayonnaise	2 tablespoons mayonnaise	2–3 tablespoons mayonnaise
1 teaspoon horseradish cream	1 teaspoon horseradish cream	1 teaspoon horseradish cream

Hard boil the eggs, halve lengthways. Remove the yolks, mash and mix with the pâté. Spoon the pâté mixture into the egg whites and arrange the halved eggs, cut-side downwards, on the lettuce leaves. Garnish with wedges of tomato and fans of gherkin (see sketch). Blend the mayonnaise and horseradish cream and spoon over the eggs.

To vary
Smoked trout or smoked salmon may be used in place of pâté.

Use a small quantity of cooked or canned salmon, or sardines and lemon juice in place of horseradish cream.

Cheese Pâté

No cooking
Serves: 4
(more if a second pâté is made to serve with this)
To store: in a cool place for 2–3 weeks. Cover with foil or melted butter.

MENU
Cheese Pâté
Stuffed Chicken Hotpot (*page 46*) with Green Vegetable
Baked Apples (*page 67*)

To freeze: cover well. Use within 4–6 weeks.

This is ideal for sandwich fillings, or excellent as an hors d'oeuvre (serve with hot toast, butter and lemon).

IMPERIAL	METRIC	AMERICAN
4 oz. Roquefort, Gorgonzola, Danish Blue *or* other veined cheese	100 g. Roquefort, Gorgonzola, Danish Blue *or* other veined cheese	4 oz. Roquefort, Gorgonzola, Danish Blue *or* other veined cheese
2 oz. butter	50 g. butter	¼ cup butter
shake cayenne pepper	shake cayenne pepper	shake cayenne pepper
pinch salt	pinch salt	pinch salt

Put the cheese into a basin and add the rest of the ingredients. Beat well. Serve in a small container.

If any is left over
Add a little lemon juice or sherry, or a few drops of Tabasco sauce, to change the flavour slightly.

Stuffed Artichokes

Cooking time: 25–30 minutes
Serves: 2
To store: make the stuffing earlier and store for several hours, but serve the artichokes when freshly cooked.
It is worthwhile cooking extra artichokes to serve cold with an oil and vinegar dressing, see under *To vary.*

MENU
Stuffed Artichokes
Herbed Omelette with Creamed Potatoes
Strawberry Ice Cream

Do *not freeze.*

IMPERIAL	METRIC	AMERICAN
2 globe artichokes	2 globe artichokes	2 globe artichokes
seasoning	seasoning	seasoning
2 oz. cooked ham	50 g. cooked ham	2 oz. cooked ham
4–6 canned anchovy fillets*	4–6 canned anchovy fillets*	4–6 canned anchovy fillets*
2 tablespoons soft breadcrumbs	2 tablespoons soft breadcrumbs	2–3 tablespoons soft bread crumbs
2 tablespoons grated Parmesan cheese	2 tablespoons grated Parmesan cheese	2–3 tablespoons grated Parmesan cheese
2 oz. butter	50 g. butter	¼ cup butter

* page 65 gives a recipe to use up the left-over anchovy fillets.

Trim the stalks and tips of the leaves from the artichokes and cook in boiling, well seasoned, water for about 25 minutes until tender. Drain carefully and pull away the centre, put the stuffing into this cavity. Heat for 5 minutes only in a moderate to moderately hot oven, 375–400°F (190–200°C), Gas Mark 5–6. Serve with the melted butter.
   To make the stuffing: chop the ham and anchovy fillets, mix with the crumbs, cheese and seasoning.

To vary
Cook the artichokes as above, remove the centres while warm. Allow the artichokes to cool. Fill the centres with oil and vinegar dressing.

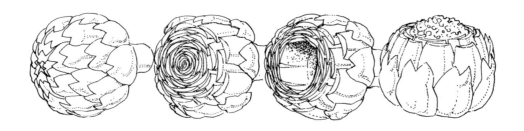

MAKING SOUPS

It is hardly worthwhile cooking an *elaborate* soup for two people, especially when ready-prepared 'convenience' soups are so varied and good in quality. You can produce interesting, unusual and economical soups though quite easily, and I have given some recipes that can be used as a basis for variation, and which are not available as canned or dehydrated soups.

Do not waste cooked vegetables; most of them make good cream of vegetable soup (see page 14). If you have any left-over brown stock make an onion soup, see below.

Clear Onion Soup

Cooking time: 20–26 minutes
Serves: 2
To store: in a cool place.

To freeze: cook, freeze and use within 2–3 months.

IMPERIAL	METRIC	AMERICAN
2 large onions	2 large onions	2 large onions
1 oz. butter	25 g. butter	2 tablespoons butter
1 pint good brown stock	6 dl. good brown stock	2½ cups good brown stock

Slice the onions and fry in the hot butter for 5–6 minutes. Add the stock and simmer for 15–20 minutes. Season well if the stock has not been seasoned.

Cucumber Soup

No cooking
Serves: 2
To store: for 24 hours only in the refrigerator.

MENU
Cucumber Soup
Fish Kebabs with Tomato Sauce
(*page 24*)
New *or* Creamed Potatoes
Cauliflower
Fresh Fruit

Do *not freeze.*

IMPERIAL	METRIC	AMERICAN
1 small onion	1 small onion	1 small onion
½ small cucumber	½ small cucumber	½ small cucumber
5 fl. oz. (¼ pint) carton yoghourt	125 g. (⅛ litre–1½ dl.) carton yoghourt	5 fl. oz. (⅔ cup) yogurt
½ teaspoon curry powder	½ teaspoon curry powder	½ teaspoon curry powder
2 teaspoons lemon juice	2 teaspoons lemon juice	2 teaspoons lemon juice
seasoning	seasoning	seasoning
generous ¼ pint milk	generous ⅛ litre (nearly 2 dl.) milk	1 cup milk
to garnish	*to garnish*	*to garnish*
chopped chives	chopped chives	chopped chives
chopped parsley	chopped parsley	chopped parsley

Peel and grate the onion and cucumber into a basin, add the rest of the ingredients. Chill thoroughly. Spoon into the soup cups and top with chives and parsley.

To vary
Omit the curry powder and flavour the soup with chopped fresh mint, or dill or basil.

Avocado Pear Soup

Cooking time: 15 minutes
Servès: 4, or 2 for two different meals
To store: in the refrigerator for up to 2 days.

MENU
Avocado Pear Soup
Chicken Croquettes (*page 47*)
Sauté Potatoes
Tomatoes
Orange and Wine Compote (*page 68*)

Do *not freeze.*

IMPERIAL	METRIC	AMERICAN
1 onion	1 onion	1 onion
1 oz. butter *or* margarine	25 g. butter *or* margarine	2 tablespoons butter *or* margarine
1 pint chicken stock *or* water and 2 chicken stock cubes	6 dl. chicken stock *or* water and 2 chicken stock cubes	2½ cups chicken stock *or* water and 2 chicken bouillon cubes
1 large avocado pear	1 large avocado pear	1 large avocado pear
juice ½ lemon	juice ½ lemon	juice ½ lemon
seasoning	seasoning	seasoning
¼ pint thick cream	⅛ litre (1½ dl.) thick cream	⅔ cup whipping cream

Chop the onion, toss in the hot butter or margarine for 5 minutes, then add the stock or water and stock cubes, together with the skinned diced avocado pear, lemon juice and seasoning. Simmer for nearly 10 minutes; sieve or emulsify. Put *half* the soup on one side, cool and blend with *half* the cream. Cover and store, ready to serve cold (see below). Heat the rest of the soup with the remainder of the cream and serve hot.

To make a second meal
Add a pinch of curry powder and a few drops of Tabasco sauce to the cold soup. Top with chopped chives and parsley before serving.

Green Pepper Soup

Cooking time: 40 minutes
Serves: 4–6
To store: in a cool place for 2–3 days.

MENU
Green Pepper Soup
Fried Fish, etc. (*page 16*)
Caramelled Apples and Oranges
(*page 69*)

To freeze: this freezes better if cornflour (cornstarch) is used instead of flour in thickening the soup. Use half quantity only.

IMPERIAL	METRIC	AMERICAN
2 green peppers	2 green peppers	2 green peppers
2 onions	2 onions	2 onions
2 oz. butter	50 g. butter	¼ cup butter
1 pint chicken stock	6 dl. chicken stock	2½ cups chicken stock
seasoning	seasoning	seasoning
1 oz. flour	25 g. flour	¼ cup flour
¼ pint thick cream	1½ dl. thick cream	⅔ cup whipping cream
to garnish	*to garnish*	*to garnish*
chopped chives and/or chopped parsley	chopped chives and/or chopped parsley	chopped chives and/or chopped parsley

This is a good party soup.

Dice the green peppers, discard cores and most of the seeds. Keep a few seeds if you want the mixture to be a little peppery. Dice the onions, toss them with the peppers in the hot butter for about 5 minutes. Add most of the chicken stock, season well, cover the pan and simmer for approximately 30 minutes. Rub the mixture through a sieve, return to the pan. Blend the flour with remaining stock, stir into the soup. If it is a little thick at this stage, dilute with more stock or with a little milk. Add the thick cream just before serving and warm gently. Taste and re-season if required. Garnish with chives and/or parsley.

To make a second meal
a) Serve as a sauce over fried chicken portions.
b) Make it into a *Chicken Fricassée:* either use cooked chicken or simmer chicken joints in a little water and seasoning; dice the cooked chicken, add to the green pepper mixture and heat without boiling.

Budget Soups

Many foods can be used for inexpensive soups, e.g. inexpensive white fish, a small quantity of freshly minced beef, 1 portion of chicken and seasonal vegetables. Add extra food value by using milk in the ingredients where possible, and top the soup with a little grated cheese. All the soups below can be sieved or emulsified to give a smooth purée.

Irish Milk Soup: boil 2 medium sized peeled diced potatoes and 1 peeled diced onion in ¼ pint (1½ dl.–⅔ cup) boiling, well seasoned, water until tender. Sieve or emulsify. Put back into the saucepan with ½ pint (3 dl.–1¼ cups) milk and a tiny knob of butter or margarine. Heat, season well and top with chopped parsley.

To vary
Use 3 carrots or 4 Jerusalem artichokes or a mixture of root vegetables instead of potatoes.

Cream of Cabbage Soup: make a thin sauce with 1 oz. (25 g.–2 tablespoons) margarine, 1 oz. (25 g.–¼ cup) flour and ¾ pint (4½ dl.–2 cups) milk. Season well. Meanwhile, shred about a quarter of a small cabbage and cook for 3 minutes only in a little boiling salted water. Add to the sauce and heat gently.

To vary
Use sprigged cauliflower, sliced mushrooms, or a little fresh or frozen spinach in place of cabbage. Use other cooked vegetables in place of shredded cabbage.

Fish Soup: simmer about 4 oz. (100 g.) neatly diced skinned white fish and a tiny grated onion in a little seasoned water. Add to the sauce and heat gently.

Cream of Beef Soup: make a sauce as the recipe for Cream of cabbage soup but use half milk and half stock, or water and ½ beef stock (bouillon) cube. Add 3–4 oz. (75–100 g.) freshly minced raw beef, 1 small finely chopped onion, 1 stalk celery, diced. Stir well to break up the pieces of meat and cook for about 45 minutes.

Cream of Chicken Soup: use 1 small raw chicken joint, dice the meat finely and cook as the recipe above. You can also use the diced flesh from a pigeon instead. Since these game birds are surprisingly 'meaty', double the amount of sauce and make this with half milk and half stock for a more robust flavour. The soup then serves 4 instead of 2.

Cooked meat, chicken and game can be used in this soup. Make the sauce as the recipe, add the minced or chopped meat, etc., then heat for a few minutes.

Canned Soups Plus

Canned, or dehydrated soups offer a splendid variety of flavours. Make them individual though by adding extra seasoning, herbs, etc.

Many firms produce small cans of soup, and you also can use part of a packet of dehydrated soup, then store the remainder to use on a future occasion.

Some types of canned soup are available in larger sizes only and the recipes on this page suggest a way in which you can produce two different dishes from one basic soup.

Some left-over soups make good sauces–tomato and mushroom soups are the most suitable.

Many soups are quite good if served cold, so serve half the can as a hot soup, then chill the remainder, and serve on another day topped with a little yoghourt and chopped herbs.

Turtle Soup Indienne

Cooking time: 8 minutes
Serves: 2
To store: in a cool place for 1–2 days.

MENU
Turtle Soup Indienne
Ham and Potato Pancakes (*page 39*)
with Salad
Fresh Fruit

To freeze: can be frozen successfully.
Use within 2 months.

IMPERIAL	METRIC	AMERICAN
small can *or* ½ large can turtle soup	small can *or* ½ large can turtle soup	small can *or* ½ large can turtle soup
1 teaspoon curry powder	1 teaspoon curry powder	1 teaspoon curry powder
2 tablespoons thick cream	2 tablespoons thick cream	2–3 tablespoons whipping cream
½ teaspoon paprika	½ teaspoon paprika	½ teaspoon paprika

Heat the soup and curry powder. Pour into two heatproof soup cups. Top with the cream and heat under the grill (broiler) until the cream darkens slightly. Sprinkle with paprika.

To vary
Use canned consommé instead of turtle soup.

Jellied Turtle Soup

Cooking time: 2–3 minutes
Serves: 2
To store: in a cool place.

MENU
Jellied Turtle Soup
Fish Cream (*page 21*)
New *or* Creamed Potatoes
Cauliflower
Fruit Pancakes (*page 70*)

To freeze: as above.

IMPERIAL	METRIC	AMERICAN
small can *or* ½ large can turtle soup	small can *or* ½ large can turtle soup	small can *or* ½ large can turtle soup
1 level teaspoon gelatine (poor measure)	1 level teaspoon gelatine (poor measure)	1 level teaspoon gelatin (poor measure)
1 tablespoon sherry	1 tablespoon sherry	1 tablespoon sherry
½ lemon	½ lemon	½ lemon

Chop the tiny pieces of turtle from the soup. Heat the soup; soften the gelatine in the sherry, stir into the soup and stir until dissolved. Cool, add the chopped turtle flesh. Allow to set, whisk and spoon into two soup cups. Top with sliced lemon.

To vary
Use tomato juice instead of turtle soup.

FISH DISHES

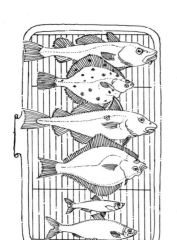

THERE IS AN EXCELLENT SELECTION OF FISH FROM WHICH TO CHOOSE
White fish – cod, fresh haddock, plaice, whiting and hake are some of the most plentiful.
Oily fish – herrings are the most economical, and salmon the most luxurious.
Shellfish – much of which, oysters, lobster, prawns and crab are fairly expensive, but mussels and scallops are more reasonable.
Fresh water fish is not easy to buy except for trout.

Be careful when buying any fish – the eyes should be bright, the flesh firm and there should be no smell of ammonia.

The recipes use a variety of fish in quick and simple dishes.

Frozen fish can often be used in the recipes, and it is possible to buy small packets of frozen fish. When once frozen fish is defrosted it must be used as soon as possible. Many types of frozen fish can be cooked *without* defrosting: i.e. the trout, shown on page 19.

Fried Fish

Cooking time: 5–8 minutes
Serves: 2
To store: in the coolest part of the refrigerator.

MENU
Green Pepper Soup (*page 13*)
Fried Fish with Fried (French Fries)
or Creamed Potatoes
Cauliflower *or* other Vegetable
Tartare Sauce (*page 50*)
Caramelled Apples and Oranges
(*page 69*)

To freeze: you can coat the fish, then freeze it if wished.

Washing-up tip: clean out the pan with kitchen paper before washing-up.

This is one of the best-liked forms of serving fish.

The method of frying fish at home is given below, but if you are short of time and buy ready-fried fish remember to reheat this on an uncovered ovenproof dish or tin. Make sure the oven is moderately hot so that you heat the fish quickly.

IMPERIAL	METRIC	AMERICAN
2 portions of fish (fillets *or* cutlets)	2 portions of fish (fillets *or* cutlets)	2 portions of fish (fillets *or* steaks)
2–3 teaspoons flour	2–3 teaspoons flour	2–3 teaspoons flour
seasoning	seasoning	seasoning
1 small egg	1 small egg	1 small egg
2 tablespoons crisp breadcrumbs (raspings)	2 tablespoons crisp breadcrumbs (raspings)	2–3 tablespoons crisp bread crumbs (raspings)
for frying	*for frying*	*for frying*
1½–2 oz. fat	40–50 g. fat	3 tablespoons-¼ cup shortening

Wash and dry the fish. Mix the flour with a little seasoning and coat the fish with this, then with the beaten egg and breadcrumbs. Pat the crumbs into the fish with a palette knife to make sure they adhere firmly. Heat the fat in the pan and cook the fish quickly on either side to brown, then lower the heat and cook through to the centre. Fillets take about 5 minutes but thicker cutlets up to 8 minutes.

Haddock Ramekins

Cooking time: 20 minutes
Serves: 2
To store: the fish can be pre-cooked, flaked and put into the dishes and kept *covered* in the refrigerator for several hours. Add the filling just before cooking.

MENU
Haddock Ramekins
Creamed Spinach, or serve this as a quick snack with Fresh Rolls and Butter.

Do *not freeze.*

IMPERIAL	METRIC	AMERICAN
8 oz. uncooked smoked haddock *or* smoked cod	200 g. uncooked smoked haddock *or* smoked cod	8 oz. uncooked smoked haddock *or* smoked cod
¼ pint milk	⅛ litre (1½ dl.) milk	⅔ cup milk
3 tablespoons thick cream	3 tablespoons thick cream	3–4 tablespoons whipping cream
seasoning	seasoning	seasoning
2 tomatoes	2 tomatoes	2 tomatoes
2 eggs	2 eggs	2 eggs
½ oz. butter	15 g. butter	1 tablespoon butter

Divide the fish into neat pieces and poach for nearly 10 minutes in the milk. Flake the fish, mix with any milk left in the pan and with half the cream. Season lightly. Slice the tomatoes, put into two shallow ovenproof dishes. Add seasoning, then the fish mixture. Break an egg on top of the fish, coat with the rest of the cream. Add seasoning and butter. Bake for 10 minutes towards the top of a hot oven, 425–450°F (220–230°C), Gas Mark 6–7.

Seafood Risotto

Cooking time: 25 minutes
Serves: 2
This is better eaten as soon as it is cooked.

MENU
Fresh Tomato Salad (*page 60*)
Seafood Risotto
Yoghourt Fool (*page 68*)

Do *not freeze.*

IMPERIAL	METRIC	AMERICAN
2 oz. mushrooms	50 g. mushrooms	½ cup mushrooms
1 onion (*optional*)	1 onion (*optional*)	1 onion (*optional*)
1 green pepper	1 green pepper	1 green pepper
2 tablespoons oil	2 tablespoons oil	2–3 tablespoons oil
3 oz. long grain rice	75 g. long grain rice	½ cup long grain rice
½ pint water	3 dl. water	1¼ cups water
seasoning	seasoning	seasoning
8 oz. white fish	200 g. white fish	8 oz. lean fish
2 oz. shelled shrimps *or* other shellfish	50 g. shelled shrimps *or* other shellfish	⅓ cup shelled shrimp *or* other shellfish
1 tablespoon chopped parsley	1 tablespoon chopped parsley	1 tablespoon chopped parsley

Slice the vegetables neatly, discard the core and seeds from the pepper. Toss in the hot oil for 3–4 minutes. Add the rice and mix with the oil and vegetables, then pour in the water. Season lightly, bring the liquid to the boil, stir briskly then lower the heat and simmer for 5 minutes. Meanwhile, dice the fish, add to the rice, cook for another 5 minutes, then stir in the shrimps or other shellfish and parsley.

To vary
Add 2 or 3 chopped anchovy fillets and 1 or 2 skinned sliced tomatoes to the mixture.

Top with grated cheese before serving.

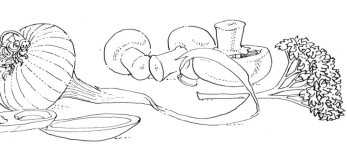

Hotpot Portuguese

Cooking time: 50 minutes
Serves: 2
To store: prepare everything but the potatoes (which will discolour if prepared beforehand).

MENU
Liver and Tongue Pâté (*page 10*)
Hotpot Portuguese with Creamed Spinach
Caramelled Banana Slices (*page 69*)

Do *not freeze* – the potatoes lose their texture.

IMPERIAL	METRIC	AMERICAN
2 cutlets (slices) of cod *or* other firm fish	2 cutlets (slices) of cod *or* other firm fish	2 steaks (slices) of cod *or* other firm fish
2 large tomatoes	2 large tomatoes	2 large tomatoes
2 oz. mushrooms	50 g. mushrooms	½ cup mushrooms
2 large potatoes	2 large potatoes	2 large potatoes
seasoning	seasoning	seasoning
2–3 teaspoons chopped chives	2–3 teaspoons chopped chives	2–3 teaspoons chopped chives
¼ pint milk	⅛ litre (1½ dl.) milk	⅔ cup milk

Cut the fish into small pieces. Skin and slice the tomatoes and chop the mushrooms fairly finely. Peel the potatoes and cut into *very thin* slices. Put the tomatoes into a shallow casserole, season well, top with the fish, mushrooms and chopped chives. Add seasoning then the potatoes, which should be arranged in a neat design. Add seasoning and the milk. Do not cover. Bake for 50 minutes in the centre of a very moderate oven, 325°F (170°C), Gas Mark 3.

Scallops and Bacon en Brochette

Cooking time: 8 minutes
Serves: 2
To store: prepare and keep in the refrigerator for several hours only.

MENU
Serve with a good Green *or* Mixed Salad as a light meal.

To freeze: as shellfish is highly perishable I would not freeze this dish.

IMPERIAL	METRIC	AMERICAN
2 scallops	2 scallops	2 scallops
seasoning	seasoning	seasoning
2 rashers streaky bacon	2 rashers streaky bacon	2 slices streaky bacon
4 button mushrooms	4 button mushrooms	4 button mushrooms
1 oz. butter	25 g. butter	2 tablespoons butter

Wash, dry and season the scallops and halve neatly. Remove the rinds from the bacon and halve each rasher. Wrap the bacon pieces round the scallops, put on long metal skewers with the mushrooms. Brush with melted butter and cook under a pre-heated grill (broiler) until the fish is tender. Turn two or three times during cooking.

To vary
Creamed Scallops: simmer the scallops in a little milk, until tender. Lift on to the scallop shells. Thicken the milk in the pan with a small amount of cornflour (cornstarch), add a knob of butter, stir until smooth over a gentle heat. Spoon over the scallops.

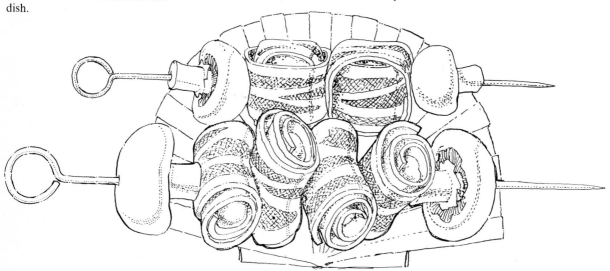

Trout with almonds, see recipe on page 20

Grilled Fish

Choose: cutlets or fillets of white (lean) fish or whole small whiting, herrings, trout and cutlets of salmon.

Pre-heat the grill (broiler) and brush the rack with a little oil, or melted butter or margarine, to prevent the fish sticking, or put a piece of foil over the rack and spread this with oil, butter or margarine. (By using foil you retain the fish juices and lessen washing-up.)

Season the fish, put it on to the rack or foil, and brush or spread with oil, butter or margarine.

You can give extra flavour by adding a little lemon juice.

Cook under the hot grill (broiler) until tender, baste well with oil, butter or margarine during cooking.

Fish Meunière

Page 16 gives one way of frying fish, but Fish Meunière is a simple way of cooking fish in a frying pan. It is particularly suitable for plaice, sole or trout.

Wash, dry and season the fish. Heat a generous amount of butter or margarine in the pan, add the fish, cook until tender. Lift out of the pan, keep hot, then add chopped parsley and/or capers and a squeeze of lemon juice or a few drops of vinegar to the butter or margarine left in the pan. Heat this–you can heat until golden brown. Pour over the hot fish, garnish and serve.

Trout with Almonds: fry blanched almonds with the fish in the butter, which should not be allowed to become brown. Serve with a mustard-flavoured mayonnaise as a sauce, see picture page 19.

Trout in Lemon Cream Sauce

Cooking time: 35–40 minutes
Serves: 2
Serve as soon as cooked.

MENU
Pâté Stuffed Eggs (*page 10*)
Trout in Lemon Cream Sauce with Hot Cucumber (*page 60*)
Green Salad
Jacket Potatoes
Fresh Fruit

To freeze: trout freeze excellently; they can be grilled (broiled) or fried from the frozen state, but in this recipe they need defrosting before preparing

IMPERIAL	METRIC	AMERICAN
2 large *or* 4 small trout	2 large *or* 4 small trout	2 large *or* 4 small trout
1 rasher bacon	1 rasher bacon	1 slice bacon
2 tablespoons soft breadcrumbs	2 tablespoons soft breadcrumbs	2–3 tablespoons soft bread crumbs
½ lemon	½ lemon	½ lemon
seasoning	seasoning	seasoning
1½ oz. butter	40 g. butter	3 tablespoons butter
4 tablespoons thick cream	4 tablespoons thick cream	5 tablespoons whipping cream
1 egg yolk	1 egg yolk	1 egg yolk
to garnish	*to garnish*	*to garnish*
parsley	parsley	parsley

Remove the heads and slit the trout along the stomachs. Remove the backbones. Chop the bacon very finely (kitchen scissors are best). Mix with the breadcrumbs, grated lemon rind, seasoning and half the butter. Fill the trout with the stuffing, fold over so they are their original shape. Put into a buttered dish, top with the rest of the butter and bake for 35 minutes (for small trout) or 40 minutes (for the larger ones) in the centre of a very moderate to moderate oven, 350–375°F (180–190°C), Gas Mark 4–5. Do not cover the dish. Meanwhile, put the cream, egg yolk, seasoning and lemon juice into a basin. Whisk over a pan of hot, but not boiling, water until smooth and slightly thickened. Lift the trout on to a serving dish, spoon the fish juice into the cream sauce, whisk to blend, then spoon over the fish. Garnish with parsley and serve.

Budget Fish Dishes

Herrings–and the fish derived from herrings, i.e. kippers, bloaters, etc. *Sprats*–these are particularly suitable for children and older people as they are so easily digested. *Baked Sprats:* wash and dry the fish and cut off the heads. Put the fish on to a well greased and heated baking tin or oven-proof dish, season lightly and brush with melted margarine. Bake for only 12–15 minutes towards the top of a moderately hot to hot oven, 400–425°F (200–220°C), Gas Mark 6–7. Serve with lemon.

Buy about 1 lb. (½ kilo) fish for two good portions.
Cod, fresh haddock and *hake* are among the cheaper and most easily available white fish.

Try fresh cod's roe or soft herring roes for a light and very nutritious meal. *Fried Cod's Roe:* this is delicious for supper or breakfast. Buy about 8 oz. (200 g.) cooked cod's roe (or a can of cod's roe). Slice neatly, dust in seasoned flour then fry in hot margarine until golden brown. This is especially good fried or grilled (broiled) with bacon. *Creamed Herring Roes:* buy about 8 oz. (200 g.) soft roes. Wash and dry. Simmer in a little seasoned milk for 5–6 minutes. Serve on hot toast or creamed potatoes.

Fish Cream

Cooking time: 15 minutes
Serves: 2
To store: in a refrigerator for 24 hours only. If storing, make the sauce a little thinner than the recipe, to allow for evaporation during storage and reheating.

MENU
Jellied Turtle Soup (*page 15*)
Fish Cream
New *or* Creamed Potatoes
Cauliflower *or* Hot Beetroot (*page 60*)
Fruit Pancakes (*page 70*)

To freeze: freezes well. Use within 1 month.

IMPERIAL	METRIC	AMERICAN
8 oz. cooked white fish (e.g. cod)	200 g. cooked white fish (e.g. cod)	8 oz. cooked lean fish (e.g. cod)
1 oz. butter *or* margarine	25 g. butter *or* margarine	2 tablespoons butter *or* margarine
1 oz. flour	25 g. flour	¼ cup flour
¼ pint milk	⅛ litre (1½ dl.) milk	⅔ cup milk
1 teaspoon lemon juice	1 teaspoon lemon juice	1 teaspoon lemon juice
seasoning	seasoning	seasoning
few drops anchovy essence	few drops anchovy essence	few drops anchovy essence
2 tablespoons thin cream	2 tablespoons thin cream	2–3 tablespoons coffee cream
2 tablespoons soft breadcrumbs	2 tablespoons soft breadcrumbs	2–3 tablespoons soft bread crumbs
2 tablespoons grated cheese	2 tablespoons grated cheese	2–3 tablespoons grated cheese

Flake the fish. Make a thick sauce with the butter or margarine, flour and milk. Add the lemon juice, seasoning, anchovy essence, cream and fish. Spoon into a heatproof dish. Top with the crumbs and cheese and brown under the grill (broiler).

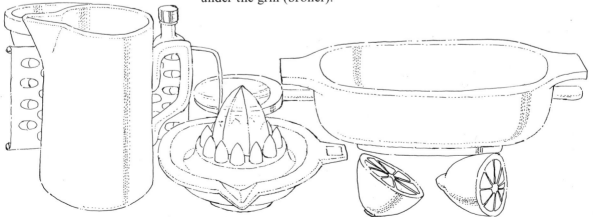

Spiced Herrings

Cooking time: 15 minutes
Serves: 2
To store: in a cool place. Although quantities are for 2 servings only, it is worthwhile preparing a larger quantity to serve any left over cold with salad.

MENU
Spiced Herrings and Green Salad
Caramel Custard (*page 72*)

To freeze: these freeze well. Use within 6–8 weeks.

IMPERIAL	METRIC	AMERICAN
4 small *or* 2 large herrings	4 small *or* 2 large herrings	4 small *or* 2 large herrings
1 apple	1 apple	1 apple
1 onion	1 onion	1 onion
1 oz. margarine	25 g. margarine	2 tablespoons margarine
½ teaspoon made-mustard	½ teaspoon made-mustard	½ teaspoon made-mustard
3 tablespoons water	3 tablespoons water	4 tablespoons water
3 tablespoons vinegar	3 tablespoons vinegar	4 tablespoons vinegar
½ teaspoon mixed spice	½ teaspoon mixed spice	½ teaspoon mixed spice
½ teaspoon mixed pickling spice seasoning	½ teaspoon mixed pickling spice seasoning	½ teaspoon mixed pickling spice seasoning

Remove the heads and bone the herrings (see below). Divide each fish into 2 fillets. Roll these fillets, put into a large shallow pan with sliced, cored (but not peeled) apple, chopped onion (skinned), and the rest of the ingredients. Simmer *steadily* for 15 minutes.

To vary
Cider Herrings: substitute sweet cider in place of the water and vinegar.

Sweet and Sour Herrings: follow the recipe for Spiced herrings, but add a little brown sugar or honey to the vinegar and water, together with about ½ tablespoon soy sauce.

Mackerel, fresh trout or cutlets (steaks) of a firm white (lean) fish can be cooked in the same way as the Spiced herrings above. Allow a slightly longer cooking time for mackerel, but a slightly shorter cooking time for trout or white fish.

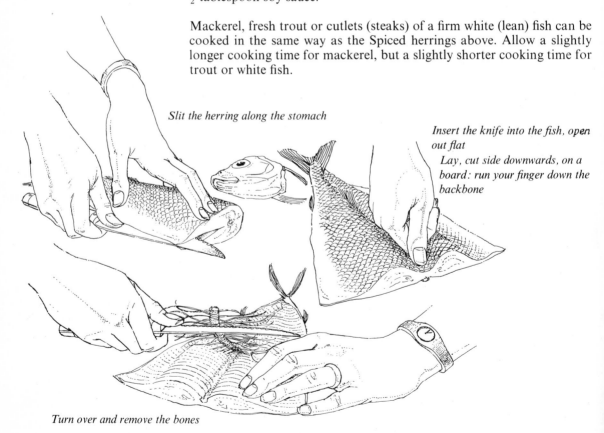

Slit the herring along the stomach

Insert the knife into the fish, open out flat
Lay, cut side downwards, on a board: run your finger down the backbone

Turn over and remove the bones

Ham rolls, see recipe on page 64

Fish Kebabs

Cooking time: 8–10 minutes
Serves: 2
To store: put fish, etc., on the skewers. Cover and keep in the refrigerator until ready to cook.

MENU
Cucumber Soup (*page 12*)
Fish Kebabs with Tomato Sauce
New *or* Creamed Potatoes
Fresh Fruit

Do *not* freeze.

IMPERIAL	METRIC	AMERICAN
8 oz. firm white fish (weight without bones)–choose cod *or* hake	200 g. firm white fish (weight without bones)–choose cod *or* hake	8 oz. firm lean fish (weight without bones)–choose cod *or* hake
2–4 tiny firm tomatoes	2–4 tiny firm tomatoes	2–4 tiny firm tomatoes
a few small mushrooms	a few small mushrooms	a few small mushrooms
1 oz. butter *or* margarine	25 g. butter *or* margarine	2 tablespoons butter *or* margarine
seasoning	seasoning	seasoning
1 lemon	1 lemon	1 lemon

Cut the fish into neat pieces. Put on to two skewers with the tomatoes and mushrooms. Brush with melted butter or margarine, season lightly and flavour with the juice from one-third of the lemon. Cook under a preheated grill (broiler) for 8–10 minutes, turning several times. Serve with rings of lemon, or with quick Tomato sauce, as below.

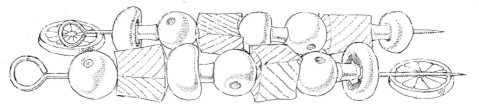

Tomato Sauce

Cooking time: see method
Serves: 2
To store: in the refrigerator.

To freeze: either freeze a concentrated tomato purée and dilute with water as the recipe on right, or freeze the sauce.

IMPERIAL	METRIC	AMERICAN
2 large ripe tomatoes	2 large ripe tomatoes	2 large ripe tomatoes
$\frac{1}{4}$ pint water	$\frac{1}{8}$ litre ($1\frac{1}{2}$ dl.) water	$\frac{2}{3}$ cup water
few drops Worcestershire sauce	few drops Worcestershire sauce	few drops Worcestershire sauce
seasoning	seasoning	seasoning
shake garlic salt	shake garlic salt	shake garlic salt

Skin and chop the tomatoes. Put into a saucepan with the rest of the ingredients and simmer until a smooth purée. There is no need to sieve this, but you could emulsify it in the liquidiser (blender) if wished.

Note. Cook a larger quantity. Store any surplus, reheat adding other ingredients or flavours, so the sauce does not become monotonous, e.g. add chopped bacon and onion, Tabasco sauce, etc.

Economical Quickies

Fish Cakes: blend almost equal quantities of cooked flaked fish and creamed potatoes. Bind with a little beaten egg or a small quantity of left-over white sauce. Form into flat cakes, coat in seasoned flour, or flour then beaten egg and crumbs, and fry until crisp and brown.

Fish au Gratin: put cooked flaked fish into a white or cheese sauce, page 50. Top with breadcrumbs and a little margarine, and crisp under the grill (broiler).

Fish Pie: use left-over cooked fish in the recipe on page 25. You can heat this in a white or cheese sauce, page 50, or you can use a small can of cream of mushroom, cream of tomato or cream of asparagus soup. To make a more filling fish pie, top with mashed potatoes instead of crushed potato crisps (chips).

Canned and Frozen Fish

Look for small cans of salmon and tuna fish to use in various dishes. Store any left in the refrigerator, and use as soon as possible.

Frozen fish is packed in small sizes, suitable for two people. Busy cooks will find that most frozen fish can be cooked from the frozen state, and the ready-coated fish saves an appreciable amount of time.

Salmon Loaf: this makes canned salmon (use the cheaper pink type) into a meal for four, or you can serve the loaf hot for two people then allow the rest to cool and serve it cold with salad. Blend 8 oz. (200 g.) flaked canned salmon with 8 oz. (200 g.–1 cup) very smooth mashed potatoes, 1 tablespoon chopped parsley, 4 oz. (100 g.) well drained canned corn, seasoning and 1 egg. Grease a 1–1½ lb. (½–¾ kilo) loaf tin, coat with crisp breadcrumbs (raspings). Put in the mixture and bake for 35 minutes in the centre of a moderate oven, 375°F (190°C), Gas Mark 4–5.

To vary
Tuna fish, cooked white fish or smoked haddock could be used instead.

Crunchy Fish Pie

Cooking time: 20 minutes
Serves: 2
To store: the filling can be prepared and kept in the refrigerator for 1 day; do not put on the crisps until ready to bake.

MENU
Avocado Vinaigrette (*page 9*)
Crunchy Fish Pie with Salad *or* a
Green Vegetable
Fresh Fruit

Do *not freeze.*

IMPERIAL	METRIC	AMERICAN
3 oz. potato crisps	75 g. potato crisps	3 oz. potato chips
2 tomatoes	2 tomatoes	2 tomatoes
small can cream of mushroom soup	small can cream of mushroom soup	small can cream of mushroom soup
small can salmon*	small can salmon*	small can salmon*
2 teaspoons chopped parsley	2 teaspoons chopped parsley	2 teaspoons chopped parsley

* the cheaper pink salmon can be used.

Crush the potato crisps lightly; they should not be too fine. Slice the tomatoes, put into the bottom of an ovenproof dish. Mix the soup with the flaked salmon and parsley. Spoon over the tomatoes. Top with the potato crisps and bake for 20 minutes above the centre of a moderate to moderately hot oven, 375–400°F (190–200°C), Gas Mark 5–6.

To vary
Change the soup used in this recipe: try cream of tomato or cream of asparagus soup.

Use canned tuna fish, or canned or frozen herring roes instead of salmon. Simmer the herring roes in the soup for a few minutes then proceed as the recipe.

MEAT DISHES

When you are short of time choose the quick cooking 'prime' cuts that can be grilled (broiled) or fried. Although comparatively expensive, there is no necessity to use elaborate cooking methods, for example try:

Escalopes of Veal: choose thin slices (fillets) of veal. Coat in beaten egg and crumbs, if wished, or fry without coating. Fry steadily in hot butter, or butter mixed with a little oil, until tender.

The garnishes can be varied, i.e. use slices of lemon or chopped parsley and/or chopped hard-boiled egg (*as the cover picture*) or anchovy fillets or fried egg.

Kebabs: tender cuts of meat, steak, pork, lamb, sausages, bacon rolls, can be used to make attractive and appetising meat kebabs. Prepare and cook as the fish kebabs on page 24, turning the kebabs several times during cooking. Serve with mixed cooked vegetables or boiled rice.

Steak Diane

See colour picture, opposite

Cooking time: from 6 minutes, see method.
Serves: 2
Serve as soon as cooked.

MENU
Smoked Salmon
Steak Diane with Salad and Sauté *or* New Potatoes
Ice Cream with Mocha Sauce (*page 66*)

To freeze: frozen steaks may be used in this recipe very successfully.

IMPERIAL	METRIC	AMERICAN
2 oz. mushrooms	50 g. mushrooms	$\frac{1}{2}$ cup mushrooms
1 onion	1 onion	1 onion
1–2 garlic cloves (*optional*)	1–2 garlic cloves (*optional*)	1–2 garlic cloves (*optional*)
2 thin fillet *or* rump steaks	2 thin fillet *or* rump steaks	2 thin fillet *or* rump beef-steaks
3 oz. butter	75 g. butter	$\frac{3}{8}$ cup butter
seasoning	seasoning	seasoning
few drops Worcestershire sauce	few drops Worcestershire sauce	few drops Worcestershire sauce
2–3 teaspoons chopped parsley	2–3 teaspoons chopped parsley	2–3 teaspoons chopped parsley
2–3 tablespoons brandy	2–3 tablespoons brandy	3–4 tablespoons brandy

Wash, dry, slice the mushrooms. Peel and chop the onion and garlic. Flatten the steaks with a rolling pin. Heat two-thirds of the butter in a large frying pan and cook the vegetables for 3 minutes; push to the sides of the pan where they will continue to cook more slowly. Heat the remaining butter and put in the steaks. If you like these very under-done, cook for 1 minute only on either side, but for a well-done steak allow 2–3 minutes on either side. Add the seasoning, sauce, parsley, then the brandy. Ignite this when it is well warmed and serve at once.

Note. If having Steak Diane for a party it is a good idea to cook all the vegetables earlier and keep them hot. Tip them into the pan *with* the raw meat so they flavour the steaks as they cook.

Mixed Grill

One of the 'consolations' of cooking for just two people is that it is possible to cook 2 steaks or fillets in one pan or under the grill (broiler) at one time, there are none of the problems of keeping food hot experienced when cooking for a big family.

The ingredients for a mixed grill vary, but the following would give a very good meal.

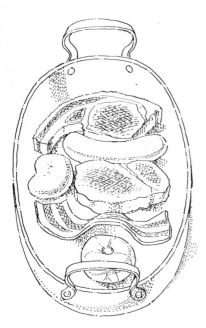

IMPERIAL	METRIC	AMERICAN
2 sausages	2 sausages	2 sausages
2 small lamb chops *or* cutlets	2 small lamb chops *or* cutlets	2 small lamb chops *or* cutlets
small piece of steak	small piece of steak	small piece beef-steak
1 *or* 2 lamb kidneys	1 *or* 2 lamb kidneys	1 *or* 2 lamb kidneys
1 oz. butter *or* margarine	25 g. butter *or* margarine	2 tablespoons butter *or* margarine
1 *or* 2 rashers bacon	1 *or* 2 rashers bacon	1 *or* 2 slices bacon

Always work out the cooking order for the food, so that everything will be ready to serve. In this menu the sausages and chops or cutlets may be put under the pre-heated grill (broiler) together. Cook for 5 minutes, turning once or twice, then add the steak (divided into two pieces) and the halved kidneys. Spread the steak and kidneys with the butter or margarine and continue cooking for another 5 minutes. Then add the bacon (halve 1 rasher) and complete the cooking.

Pork Chops with Raisin Sauce

Cooking time: 20 minutes
Serves: 2
To store: in the refrigerator for 2–3 days only. The sauce can be kept longer.

MENU
Potted Shrimps
Pork Chops with Raisin Sauce
Boiled Potatoes
Green Vegetable
Apple Ginger Creams (*page 67*)

To freeze: frozen pork chops may be cooked from the frozen state.

IMPERIAL	METRIC	AMERICAN
2 pork chops	2 pork chops	2 pork loin chops
for the sauce	*for the sauce*	*for the sauce*
1 garlic clove	1 garlic clove	1 garlic clove
1 small orange	1 small orange	1 small orange
½ pint chicken stock *or* water and ½–1 chicken stock cube	¼ litre (3 dl.) chicken stock *or* water and ½–1 chicken stock cube	1¼ cups chicken stock *or* water and ½–1 chicken bouillon cube
1 tablespoon raisins	1 tablespoon raisins	1 tablespoon raisins
2 level teaspoons cornflour	2 level teaspoons cornflour	2 level teaspoons cornstarch
seasoning	seasoning	seasoning

Grill (broil) the pork chops steadily; brown them quickly on either side, then lower the heat and continue to cook more slowly until tender (total cooking time about 15 minutes). Meanwhile, crush the clove of garlic and squeeze the juice from the orange, put into the saucepan with half the stock, or water and stock cube, and the raisins. Heat steadily. Blend the cornflour with the remaining stock or water, add to the liquid and stir well until thickened. Season well.

To vary
Use lamb chops instead of pork, or slices of bacon or gammon.

This sauce is very good with grilled (broiled) sausages or cooked frozen hamburgers.

Cooking with Bacon

Choose: gammon for luxury dishes, or back or streaky rashers (slices) for a more economical grilling (broiling) or frying bacon. Gammon, collar or forehock are suitable for boiling.

Bacon is not only an ideal breakfast food but it forms the basis of quick meals for many other occasions. If you like a mild flavour choose 'green' or sweet-cure bacon. Look for the small sized boiling joints. Check on the date, if given, to make sure the bacon has not been stored for too long a period. Simmer gently for 20–35 minutes per lb. (depending on cut). Expensive best gammon needs the shorter cooking time.

Cured bacon joints should be soaked for a minimum of 12 hours in cold water.

Gammon with Mustard and Orange Sauce

Cooking time: 12 minutes
Serves: 2
Serve as soon as cooked.

MENU
Gammon with Mustard and Orange Sauce
New *or* Creamed Potatoes
Cauliflower *or* Broccoli
Lemon Syllabub (*page 71*)

To freeze: salted and cured meats such as bacon and ham may be frozen, but use within 4–6 weeks if possible.

IMPERIAL	METRIC	AMERICAN
for the sauce	*for the sauce*	*for the sauce*
1 small orange	1 small orange	1 small orange
2 tablespoons red-currant jelly	2 tablespoons red-currant jelly	2–3 tablespoons red currant jelly
2–3 teaspoons made-mustard	2–3 teaspoons made-mustard	2–3 teaspoons made-mustard
2 gammon slices	2 gammon slices	2 slices smoked ham about ½″ thick
1 oz. butter	25 g. butter	2 tablespoons butter
2 tomatoes	2 tomatoes	2 tomatoes
seasoning	seasoning	seasoning

Squeeze the juice from the orange. Put the sauce ingredients into a basin and stand over a pan of very hot water. Meanwhile, remove the skin from the gammon (slit the fat to encourage this to brown), and grill (broil) steadily for about 10 minutes or until tender, turning during cooking. Brush with the melted butter during cooking. Add the halved seasoned tomatoes towards the end of the cooking period.

To vary
This sauce is very good with cold ham. Simply heat to dissolve the jelly, then allow to cool and serve with the ham.

Bacon and Celery Twists

Cooking time: 10 minutes
Serves: 2
To store: the canned celery hearts can be kept in the refrigerator for 1–2 days. See page 32 for Menu using the rest of the celery.

MENU
Tomato *or* Orange Juice
Bacon and Celery Twists
Cheese and Biscuits

This dish does *not freeze.*

IMPERIAL	METRIC	AMERICAN
half can celery hearts	half can celery hearts	half can celery hearts
2–4 rashers bacon*	2–4 rashers bacon*	2–4 slices bacon*
2 slices bread	2 slices bread	2 slices bread
2 eggs	2 eggs	2 eggs
seasoning	seasoning	seasoning
little butter	little butter	little butter

* if using long streaky bacon, 2 rashers (slices) may be sufficient.

Drain the celery well. Remove the rinds and twist the bacon round the celery; make sure it is well covered. Put into the pan of the grill (broiler) and cook for about 5 minutes under the grill. Put the rack in position and toast the bread; poach the eggs in seasoned water at the same time. Butter the toast. Lift the eggs on to this and put on to a dish, then lift the celery twists out of the pan and arrange with the eggs, etc.

Bacon Grill with Corn Cakes

See colour picture, opposite

Cooking time: 15 minutes
Serves: 4
Eat as soon as cooked.

MENU
Grapefruit Cocktail (*page 8*)
Bacon Grill with Corn Cakes and Salad
Asparagus Tips
Cheese and Biscuits

To freeze: there is no point in freezing the bacon grill meat as it keeps perfectly in a can. Cooked frozen corn could be used.

This will give a colourful and appetising meal for unexpected guests. The whole menu comes from the storecupboard.

IMPERIAL	METRIC	AMERICAN
for the batter	*for the batter*	*for the batter*
4 oz. flour, preferably plain	100 g. flour, preferably plain	1 cup flour, preferably all-purpose
pinch salt	pinch salt	pinch salt
1 egg	1 egg	1 egg
¼ pint milk	⅛ litre (1½ dl.) milk	⅔ cup milk
7 oz. can sweetcorn	175 g. can sweetcorn	7 oz. can kernel corn
for frying	*for frying*	*for frying*
3 oz. fat	75 g. fat	⅜ cup shortening
12 oz. can bacon grill (*or* luncheon meat)	300 g. can bacon grill (*or* luncheon meat)	12 oz. can bacon grill (*or* luncheon meat)
4 eggs	4 eggs	4 eggs
to garnish	*to garnish*	*to garnish*
(*all these are optional*)	(*all these are optional*)	(*all these are optional*)
lettuce	lettuce	lettuce
watercress	watercress	watercress
chopped parsley	chopped parsley	chopped parsley
tomatoes	tomatoes	tomatoes

Sieve the flour and salt, add the egg and milk and beat until a smooth batter. Drain the sweetcorn and mix with the batter. Heat most of the fat in the frying pan and drop large spoonfuls of the mixture into this. Cook for 2 minutes until golden brown, turn and fry for 2 minutes on the second side until brown. Lower the heat and cook for a further 3 minutes. Lift out of pan on to absorbent paper on a tin or ovenproof plate, and keep warm while completing the cooking. Slice the bacon grill, then either heat under the grill (broiler) or in the frying pan. Keep hot while cooking the eggs. Heat the remaining fat in the pan and cook the eggs. Lift on to serving dish, or four individual plates; garnish with lettuce, watercress, parsley and sliced tomatoes.

To vary
Bacon and Corn Fritters: chop about one-third of the bacon grill and add to the sweetcorn batter. This makes a complete meal with fried eggs and salad, and would leave a substantial amount of meat for another meal for two people. Use as the recipes on pages 41 and 42.

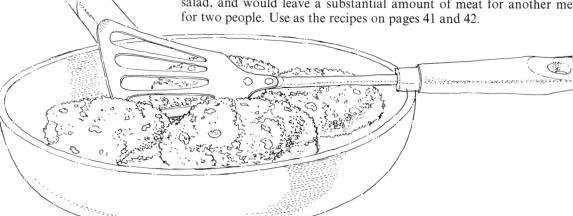

Bacon grill with corn cakes

Beef olives, see recipe on page 37

Lamb Cutlets with Curried Sauce

Cooking time: 35 minutes
Serves: 2, but some sauce left for another dish (*see page 52*)
To store: the sauce improves by being stored for 24 hours.

MENU
Tomato Juice
Lamb Cutlets with Curried Sauce and Rice
Celery Hearts
Ice Cream with Caramel Sauce (*page 66*)

To freeze: the sauce freezes well. The cutlets may be cooked from the frozen state.

IMPERIAL	METRIC	AMERICAN
for the sauce	*for the sauce*	*for the sauce*
1 small onion	1 small onion	1 small onion
1 small apple	1 small apple	1 small apple
1 oz. margarine	25 g. margarine	2 tablespoons margarine
2–3 teaspoons curry powder	2–3 teaspoons curry powder	2–3 teaspoons curry powder
1 *level* tablespoon cornflour	1 *level* tablespoon cornflour	1 *level* tablespoon cornstarch
¾ pint chicken stock *or* water and 1 chicken stock cube	⅜ litre (4½ dl.) chicken stock *or* water and 1 chicken stock cube	2 cups chicken stock *or* water and 1 chicken bouillon cube
2 oz. raisins	50 g. raisins	⅓ cup raisins
1 tablespoon chutney seasoning	1 tablespoon chutney seasoning	1 tablespoon chutney seasoning
few drops vinegar *or* lemon juice	few drops vinegar *or* lemon juice	few drops vinegar *or* lemon juice
4 lamb cutlets	4 lamb cutlets	4 lamb loin chops

Peel and grate the onion and apple, toss in the hot margarine, then add the curry powder and cook for 2–3 minutes. Blend the cornflour and stock, or water and stock cube, then add to the onion and apple mixture. Bring to the boil and cook until thickened slightly, add the rest of the ingredients. Cover the pan and leave to simmer steadily for 15 minutes and while cooking the cutlets. Grill (broil) or fry the cutlets and arrange on a dish. Coat with a little sauce. Save the rest of the sauce for the Curried eggs, page 52, or to use up left-over pieces of meat or fish which may be heated in the sauce.

Veal with Soured Cream Sauce

Cooking time: 15 minutes
Serves: 2
Serve as soon as possible after cooking.

MENU
Smoked Trout with Horseradish Cream
Veal with Soured Cream Sauce
Noodles *or* Potatoes
Courgettes
Fresh Pineapple

To freeze: veal fillets may be frozen and kept for several months. They can be cooked from the frozen state.

IMPERIAL	METRIC	AMERICAN
2 slices (escalopes) of veal	2 slices (escalopes) of veal	2 thin boneless cutlets (escalopes) of veal
1½ oz. butter	40 g. butter	3 tablespoons butter
1 teaspoon olive oil	1 teaspoon olive oil	1 teaspoon olive oil
2 oz. mushrooms	50 g. mushrooms	½ cup mushrooms
¼ pint dairy soured cream	⅛ litre (1½ dl.) dairy soured cream	⅔ cup dairy soured cream
seasoning	seasoning	seasoning
½ teaspoon paprika	½ teaspoon paprika	½ teaspoon paprika
to garnish	*to garnish*	*to garnish*
watercress	watercress	watercress

Flatten the slices of veal with a rolling pin. Heat the butter and oil in a frying pan; fry the veal for about 4 minutes on either side. Lift out of the pan and keep hot, do *NOT* allow the meat to dry. Put the sliced mushrooms into the pan and cook for 3 minutes in the juices, then stir in the soured cream, seasoning and paprika. Blend well, and heat gently. Replace the veal escalopes in the pan and heat gently in the sauce. Serve in a border of watercress.

Thin slices of lean pork (ham butt slices) could be used instead of veal.

Buying a Joint

Cooking times: roasting

Beef: 15–20 minutes per lb. and 15–20 minutes over, depending upon how well-done you like the meat.
Choose: topside, sirloin, rib.

Lamb: 20 minutes per lb. and 20 minutes over.
Choose: half or whole leg, half or whole shoulder, loin, best end of neck (an excellent small joint), breast (boned and rolled).

Pork: 25 minutes per lb. and 25 minutes over.
Choose: loin, spare-rib – leg and shoulder very large but excellent joints.

Veal: 25 minutes per lb. and 25 minutes over.
Choose: breast (boned and rolled), loin, best end of neck, fillet (cut from top of leg).

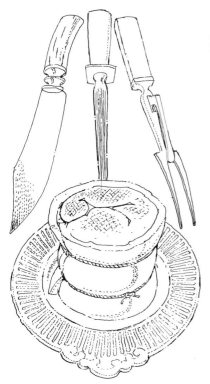

The flavour of the meat in a good joint is quite unlike that of cutlets, steaks, etc., and no doubt there are occasions when you want to buy a joint. Obviously the best time is when entertaining friends, particularly if these live alone, or there are just two of them, and they, like you, have joints fairly rarely.

This page gives ideas for using up the joint after cooking, but before considering that, check upon cooking times in the left-hand column. These times assume you are cooking the meat in a hot oven, 425–450°F (220–230°C), Gas Mark 6–7, for the first 15 minutes, then lowering it to moderate to moderately hot, 375–400°F (190–200°C), Gas Mark 5–6, for the rest of the time. You can cover the meat with foil or put it into a covered roasting tin (except for pork – see below), but in this case allow about 20 minutes extra cooking time or set the oven 25°F (10°C) or 1 Gas Mark hotter.

Lamb and pork require no extra fat, just rub the fat of pork with a little oil, this gives you the crisp 'crackling'.

Very lean beef (topside, in particular) needs a small knob of fat, but where you have a good amount of fat, as in sirloin or rib, you have no need to add fat.

Veal needs plenty of fat to keep it moist.

TO USE UP ANY COOKED MEAT

1 If you slightly under-roast the meat and carve from the outside only, you can then re-roast the meat a second time without any ill effects. Be very careful to heat the meat *thoroughly* on the first occasion, since partially cooked meat is an excellent 'breeding ground' for bacteria.

2 Cut off fairly thick slices from the joint, turn into:
Devilled Beef (*or* lamb *or* veal *or* pork): spread the meat with butter or margarine blended with a generous amount of curry powder, a few drops of Worcestershire sauce, a shake of pepper and a small amount of chutney or chopped mustard pickle. Cover with breadcrumbs, cook steadily under a pre-heated grill (broiler).

3 *Quick Stew:* make a brown sauce, see page 50; add sliced carrots, onions and any other fresh vegetables, or add a tablespoon of raisins or other dried fruit, then cook until the vegetables are nearly tender. Add the diced cooked meat and heat through – do not continue cooking, otherwise the meat toughens.

4 *Meat Curry:* make the curry sauce suggested on the opposite page, but use slightly more liquid; add the diced meat and allow to stand in the sauce overnight or for several hours, so the meat absorbs the flavour. Simmer steadily for about 30 minutes.

5 Make into some of the recipes that follow on these pages, but remember that really good cold meat is excellent with salads, or as sandwich fillings.

Savoury Meat Balls

Cooking time: 15 minutes
Serves: 4, or 2 for two meals, see
below and right
To store: in the refrigerator or a
cool place.

MENU 1
Grapefruit
Savoury Meat Balls
Creamed Spinach
Broad Beans in Piquant Sauce
(*page 48*)
Fruit Condé (*page 78*)
MENU 2
Savoury Meat Balls with Spaghetti
and Tomato Sauce
Green Salad
Cheese and Fruit

To freeze: these freeze excellently.
Fry, then either freeze in the tomato
sauce, or freeze the meat balls and
the sauce in two separate
containers. Use within 2 months.

IMPERIAL	METRIC	AMERICAN
1 onion	1 onion	1 onion
1 oz. fat	25 g. fat	2 tablespoons shortening
1 tablespoon flour	1 tablespoon flour	1 tablespoon flour
¼ pint milk	⅛ litre (1½ dl.) milk	⅔ cup milk
seasoning	seasoning	seasoning
12 oz. cooked meat	300 g. cooked meat	12 oz. cooked meat
2 oz. seedless raisins	50 g. seedless raisins	⅓ cup seedless raisins
2 oz. walnuts	50 g. walnuts	½ cup walnuts
to coat	*to coat*	*to coat*
1 egg	1 egg	1 egg
2 oz. crisp breadcrumbs (raspings)	50 g. crisp breadcrumbs (raspings)	1 cup crisp bread crumbs (raspings)
to fry	*to fry*	*to fry*
2 oz. margarine *or* butter	50 g. margarine *or* butter	¼ cup margarine *or* butter

Chop the onion very finely, fry in the hot fat, then stir in the flour and
milk. Bring the sauce to the boil, stir until thickened, then season well.
Stir in the minced meat, raisins and chopped nuts. Allow the mixture to
cool then form into small balls, see below. Coat in beaten egg and the crisp
breadcrumbs, then fry in the hot margarine or butter until crisp and brown.
Drain on absorbent paper. Serve half the balls with creamed spinach.
Store the remainder in the refrigerator.

TO MAKE ANOTHER MEAL
Make the Tomato sauce as page 24. Cook enough spaghetti for two people.
Put the spaghetti on to a hot dish. Heat the meat balls for a few minutes in
the sauce and spoon over the spaghetti.

Note. If you wish to make enough sauce for generous servings for four
people use *at least* double the quantities given on page 24.

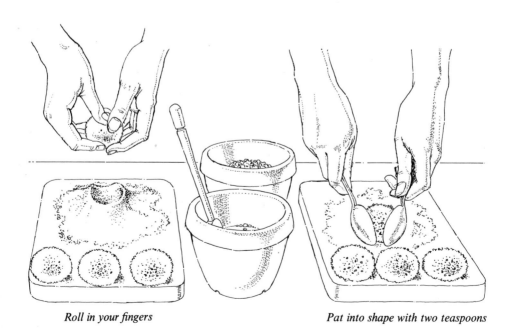

Roll in your fingers   *Pat into shape with two teaspoons*

Moussaka

Cooking time: 1½ hours
Serves: 2 (generously) but could
extend to 3 or even 4 with a
filling first course
To store: I think this dish tastes
better if stored overnight in the
refrigerator, then reheated.

MENU
Moussaka
Salad *or* Broccoli
Fresh Fruit

To freeze: this freezes very well after
cooking. The sauce has a better
texture for freezing if you use
cornflour (cornstarch) instead of
flour – use half the quantity only.

To avoid extra washing-up: make up
the cheese sauce in the frying pan
used for frying aubergine, etc.

This particular version uses left-over cooked lamb.

IMPERIAL	METRIC	AMERICAN
2 oz. margarine	50 g. margarine	¼ cup margarine
2 onions	2 onions	2 onions
1 large aubergine	1 large aubergine	1 large eggplant
8 oz. potatoes	200 g. potatoes	8 oz. potatoes
seasoning	seasoning	seasoning
8–12 oz. diced cooked lamb	200–250 g. diced cooked lamb	8–12 oz. diced cooked lamb
2 tomatoes	2 tomatoes	2 tomatoes
for the sauce	*for the sauce*	*for the sauce*
1 oz. margarine	25 g. margarine	2 tablespoons margarine
1 oz. flour	25 g. flour	¼ cup flour
¾ pint milk *or* use half milk and half stock	⅜ litre (4½ dl.) milk *or* use half milk and half stock	2 cups milk *or* use half milk and half stock
seasoning	seasoning	seasoning
3 oz. grated Cheddar cheese	75 g. grated Cheddar cheese	¾ cup grated Cheddar cheese
1 egg	1 egg	1 egg
grated nutmeg	grated nutmeg	grated nutmeg
to garnish	*to garnish*	*to garnish*
chopped parsley	chopped parsley	chopped parsley

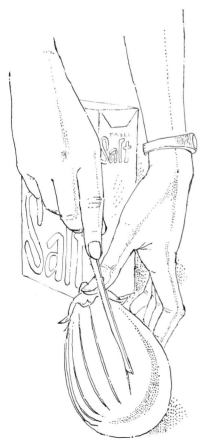

Heat the margarine and fry the thinly sliced onions in this; lift on to a plate
and turn the sliced unpeeled aubergine and peeled sliced potatoes in any
margarine that remains, season well. Mix the diced meat, onions and
skinned sliced tomatoes and seasoning. Make a pouring sauce with the
margarine, flour and liquid, season, stir in the grated cheese and beaten
egg, but do not cook again; add a little grated nutmeg. Put a potato and
aubergine layer into a casserole, then a meat layer, followed by potatoes,
meat, etc.; add a very little sauce to each layer. Fill the dish like this,
ending with a potato layer and sauce. Cover with a lid and bake for
approximately 1¼ hours (depending upon depth of casserole) in the centre
of a very moderate oven, 325–350°F (170–180°C), Gas Mark 3–4. Lift the
lid towards the end of the cooking time if you wish to brown the topping
slightly. Garnish with parsley.

To vary
Other cooked meat may be used instead of cooked lamb.
Add a little curry powder to a white sauce, omit the cheese.
Use *raw* minced meat instead of cooked meat, and allow 15–20 minutes
longer cooking time at the lower temperature above.
Economy note: use a double quantity of onions and potatoes and omit the
aubergine (eggplant).

Note. If you dislike the slightly bitter taste of aubergine (eggplant) skin,
either peel this or score the skin with a knife, sprinkle with salt and leave
for 20 minutes. The salt 'draws out' the bitterness.

Stews and casseroles

One of the most satisfying main dishes is a stew or a casserole dish. Never say these are 'dull', for a basic recipe is capable of infinite variety with the addition of various vegetables, herbs and fruits, etc. If you are short of time, cook the casserole one day, allow to cool then put into the refrigerator; reheat the next day. You will find the flavour is even better than when first made.

Veal Marengo

Cooking time: 1½ hours
Serves: 2
To store: see comments above.

MENU
Fish Pâté (*page 10*)
Veal Marengo with Peas and Noodles
Chocolate Mousse (*page 73*)

Do *not freeze* as veal loses so much of its flavour and texture.

IMPERIAL	METRIC	AMERICAN
12 oz. stewing veal	300 g. stewing veal	12 oz. stewing veal
2 tablespoons oil	2 tablespoons oil	2–3 tablespoons oil
2 oz. button mushrooms	50 g. button mushrooms	½ cup button mushrooms
6–8 tiny onions *or* shallots	6–8 tiny onions *or* shallots	6–8 tiny onions *or* shallots
1 garlic clove	1 garlic clove	1 garlic clove
½ oz. flour	15 g. flour	3 tablespoons flour
½ pint liquid, half dry white wine and half water *or* all wine *or* all water	¼ litre (3 dl.) liquid, half dry white wine and half water *or* all wine *or* all water	1¼ cups liquid, half dry white wine and half water *or* all wine *or* all water
2 teaspoons tomato purée	2 teaspoons tomato purée	2 teaspoons tomato paste
bouquet garni	bouquet garni	bouquet garni
seasoning	seasoning	seasoning

Dice the meat, toss in the hot oil, lift out, then toss the prepared mushrooms, onions or shallots and crushed garlic in the oil; remove. Add the flour and stir for 2–3 minutes, then gradually add the liquid. Bring to the boil and cook until thickened. Replace the meat and vegetables, add the tomato purée, herbs and seasoning. Cover the pan and simmer gently for 1¼ hours.

Pork Casserole

Cooking time: 1¼ hours
Serves: 2
To store: in the refrigerator before or after cooking. Reheat gently but thoroughly, see paragraph above, right.

MENU
Pork Casserole with Apple Sauce (*page 48*)
Brussels Sprouts
Baked Lemon Pudding (*page 78*)

To freeze: cook first, cool. Cover well. Use within 2 months.

IMPERIAL	METRIC	AMERICAN
2 pork chops	2 pork chops	2 pork loin chops
1 onion	1 onion	1 onion
1 dessert apple	1 dessert apple	1 dessert apple
small can tomatoes	small can tomatoes	small can tomatoes
pinch dried sage *or* ¼ teaspoon chopped fresh sage	pinch dried sage *or* ¼ teaspoon chopped fresh sage	pinch dried sage *or* ¼ teaspoon chopped fresh sage
seasoning	seasoning	seasoning
4 potatoes	4 potatoes	4 potatoes
½ oz. margarine	15 g. margarine	1 tablespoon margarine

Put the pork chops into a casserole. Add the peeled sliced onion, apple, tomatoes and liquid from the can, sage and seasoning. Peel and slice the potatoes thinly. Arrange over the meat and vegetable mixture. Season lightly and top with the margarine. Bake for 1¼ hours in the centre of a very moderate oven, 325–350°F (170–180°C), Gas Mark 3–4.

To vary
Use lamb or mutton chops, choose best end of neck for a delicious flavour or scrag end for economy.

Beef Olives

See colour picture, page 31

Cooking time: 2 hours
Serves: 4, or 2 for two meals, see below and method, right
To store: cover casserole, keep in a cool place for 1–2 days, then cook or reheat.

MENU 1
Beef Olives with Noodles and Carrots
Fruit Snow (*page 66*)

MENU 2
Curried Beef Olives with Rice and Chutney
Brussels Sprouts
Compote of Fruit (*page 66*)

To freeze: either version of the Beef Olives freezes well. Use within 2–3 months. Neither rice nor noodles freeze well.

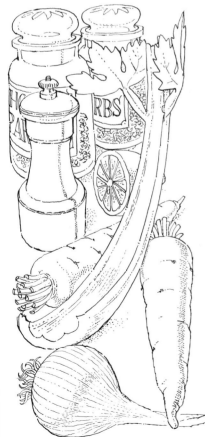

IMPERIAL	METRIC	AMERICAN
for the stuffing	*for the stuffing*	*for the stuffing*
3 oz. soft breadcrumbs	75 g. soft breadcrumbs	1 cup soft bread crumbs
1½ oz. shredded *or* chopped suet	40 g. shredded *or* chopped suet	just over ¼ cup shredded *or* chopped suet
1 tablespoon chopped parsley	1 tablespoon chopped parsley	1 tablespoon chopped parsley
pinch mixed herbs	pinch mixed herbs	pinch mixed herbs
grated rind 1 lemon	grated rind 1 lemon	grated rind 1 lemon
seasoning	seasoning	seasoning
1 egg	1 egg	1 egg
for the olives	*for the olives*	*for the olives*
1–1¼ lb. topside cut in 4 *or* 8 slices	½–⅝ kilo topside cut in 4 *or* 8 slices	1–1¼ lb. round of beef cut in 4 *or* 8 slices
1 oz. dripping *or* other fat	25 g. dripping *or* other fat	2 tablespoons dripping *or* shortening
1 onion	1 onion	1 onion
1–2 carrots	1–2 carrots	1–2 carrots
1–2 sticks celery	1–2 sticks celery	1–2 stalks celery
1 oz. flour	25 g. flour	¼ cup flour
¾ pint beef stock *or* water and 2 beef stock cubes	⅜ litre (4½ dl.) beef stock *or* water and 2 beef stock cubes	2 cups beef stock *or* water and 2 beef bouillon cubes
seasoning	seasoning	seasoning
for the curried version (MENU 2)	*for the curried version* (MENU 2)	*for the curried version* (MENU 2)
5 tablespoons extra stock *or* water	5 tablespoons extra stock *or* water	6 tablespoons extra stock *or* water
2 teaspoons curry powder	2 teaspoons curry powder	2 teaspoons curry powder
2 teaspoons raisins	2 teaspoons raisins	2 teaspoons raisins
2 teaspoons chutney	2 teaspoons chutney	2 teaspoons chutney

Mix together all the ingredients for the stuffing. If you have 4 slices of topside, flatten these with a rolling pin and halve. Spread a portion of stuffing on each piece of meat and roll securely, tie with cotton or skewer. Heat the dripping or other fat in a pan, fry the beef olives for a few minutes until golden coloured. Lift out and put on to a plate. Slice the prepared vegetables neatly and toss for 3–4 minutes in the remaining fat in the pan. Lift out on to a plate. Blend the flour with the beef stock or water and stock cubes. Pour into the pan and simmer steadily, stirring until the sauce thickens, season well.

For Menu 1: put 4 beef olives and half the vegetables into a small casserole. Cover with just over half the sauce and a lid. Cook for 1½ hours in the centre of a very moderate oven, 325°F (170°C) Gas Mark 3.

For Menu 2: blend the extra stock or water with the curry powder, pour into the sauce in the pan, bring once again to the boil, then add the raisins and chutney. Put the remaining beef olives and vegetables into a second casserole, cover with the curry sauce and foil, and store until ready to cook. Use the same cooking time as above.

The picture on page 31 shows the beef olives with noodles, etc.

Budget Meat Dishes

Meat is an expensive food, but as it is a most important source of protein most families feel it worthwhile spending a high percentage of their house-keeping money on it. Although prime quality steaks, chops, etc., are delicious to eat, they do not provide a great deal more protein than the more economical cuts of meat.

Minced beef, sausages, middle and scrag end of neck of lamb or mutton are some of the economical cuts of meat used in the recipes that follow. A recipe using tripe, which is both inexpensive and easy to digest and therefore ideal for older people, is on page 77.

Mock Duck: boil 1 medium onion in salted water, drain and chop. Divide 8 oz. (200 g.) sausagemeat into 2 portions. Flatten one portion into an oval on a heatproof dish. Mix a chopped onion, 2 tablespoons breadcrumbs, ½ tablespoon seedless raisins, 1 small peeled grated apple, seasoning and a pinch dried sage. Spoon over the sausagemeat. Take the rest of the sausage-meat and form into an oval and place over the onion mixture. Cover with greased foil. Bake for 30 minutes in the centre of a moderately hot oven, 400°F (200°C), Gas Mark 5–6. Remove the foil and continue cooking for another 10 minutes.

Pilaf of Beef: heat 1 oz. (25 g.–2 tablespoons) fat in a pan. Fry 1 chopped onion, then add 8 oz. (200 g.) minced beef and 2 tablespoons long grain rice, stir well to mix with the onion. Add ½ pint (3 dl.–1¼ cups) brown stock, or water and 1 stock (bouillon) cube. Bring the liquid to the boil, stir well, add seasoning and a pinch mixed herbs. Cover the pan, lower the heat and simmer for 20 minutes. Stir again, add 1 tablespoon chopped parsley and 2 skinned sliced tomatoes. Continue cooking gently for another 15–20 minutes.

Flemish Style Beef: heat 1 oz. (25 g.–2 tablespoons) fat in a pan. Fry 1 sliced onion and 1 sliced tomato, add 8 oz. (200 g.) minced beef and ½ pint (3 dl.–1¼ cups) beer, or use half beer and half water. Stir well, then add a good pinch mixed herbs and seasoning. Cover the pan and simmer gently for 40 minutes. Cut a small slice of white bread, remove the crusts. Spread with French mustard. Drop into the pan, heat for 5 minutes. Beat hard with a wooden spoon until the bread softens and thickens the stew.

Sweet and Sour Hamburgers: grill (broil) or fry frozen hamburgers. Meanwhile, make the sauce: blend 2 tablespoons cornflour (cornstarch) with ¼ pint (1½ dl.–⅔ cup) water. Put into a saucepan with 1 tablespoon honey, 1 tablespoon vinegar, 1 tablespoon chopped mustard pickle and 1 tablespoon sultanas. Heat steadily, stirring well. Serve over the hamburgers.

This sauce is also good with grilled (broiled) cutlets or with fish.

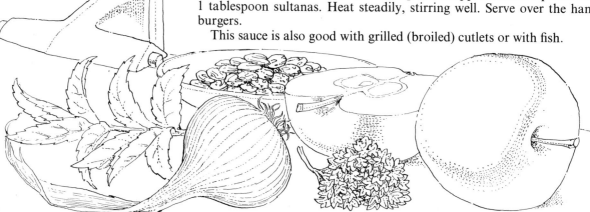

Ham and Potato Pancakes

Cooking time: 10 minutes
Serves: 2 as a main dish, or 4 as a snack
Serve as soon as cooked.

MENU
Ham and Potato Pancakes
Green Salad *or* Green Beans
Fresh Fruit Salad

Do *not freeze.*

IMPERIAL	METRIC	AMERICAN
4 oz. cooked ham	100 g. cooked ham	4 oz. cooked ham
1 onion	1 onion	1 onion
2 large potatoes	2 large potatoes	2 large potatoes
2 oz. self-raising flour*	50 g. self-raising flour*	½ cup self-rising flour*
2 eggs	2 eggs	2 eggs
seasoning	seasoning	seasoning
2 tablespoons milk	2 tablespoons milk	2–3 tablespoons milk
for frying	*for frying*	*for frying*
2 oz. fat	50 g. fat	¼ cup shortening

* or use plain (all-purpose) flour and ½ teaspoon baking powder (double acting).

Chop the ham. Peel and grate the onion and uncooked potatoes. Mix the ham, onion and potato, add the flour or flour and baking powder. Beat in eggs, seasoning and milk. Drop spoonfuls of the mixture into hot fat. Fry quickly for 2 minutes, turn, fry for 2 minutes on second side. Lower heat, cook for a further 5–6 minutes. Drain on absorbent paper; serve.

Liver and Bacon Ragoût

Cooking time: 30 minutes
Serves: 2–3 (this would be a good choice for a child's main meal, see *page 76*)

MENU
Liver and Bacon Ragoût
Brussels Sprouts *or* Cauliflower
Ice Cream

To freeze: prepare as method, right, but omit the baked beans. Freeze, and use within 4 weeks. Add the baked beans when reheating.

IMPERIAL	METRIC	AMERICAN
6 oz. calf's *or* lamb's *or* pig's liver (in one piece)	150 g. calf's *or* lamb's *or* pig's liver (in one piece)	6 oz. calf's *or* lamb's *or* pig's liver (in one piece)
3 rashers streaky bacon	3 rashers streaky bacon	3 slices streaky bacon
½ oz. fat	15 g. fat	1 tablespoon shortening
1 onion	1 onion	1 onion
good pinch mixed herbs	good pinch mixed herbs	good pinch mixed herbs
seasoning	seasoning	seasoning
pinch sugar	pinch sugar	pinch sugar
½ oz. flour	15 g. flour	2 tablespoons flour
⅜ pint (12 tablespoons) brown stock	nearly ¼ litre (2 dl.) brown stock	1 cup brown stock
½–1 teaspoon made-mustard	½–1 teaspoon made-mustard	½–1 teaspoon made-mustard
½ tablespoon tomato purée *or* tomato ketchup	½ tablespoon tomato purée *or* tomato ketchup	½ tablespoon tomato paste *or* tomato catsup
small can baked beans	small can baked beans	small can baked beans
to garnish	*to garnish*	*to garnish*
parsley *or* ½ green pepper	parsley *or* ½ green pepper	parsley *or* ½ green pepper

Cut the liver into six neat fingers; halve each bacon rasher (remove the rinds), wrap round the liver. Secure with cocktail sticks. Heat the bacon rinds and fat, remove rinds when you have extracted all the fat; fry the bacon and liver rolls for 2–3 minutes then add the chopped onion and fry for a further 2–3 minutes; add herbs and seasonings. Blend the flour with the stock, stir into the pan; bring slowly to the boil. When thickened slightly, add mustard and tomato flavouring. Cover the pan, simmer for 20 minutes; add the baked beans, heat for a few minutes. (Remove the cocktail sticks.) Garnish with parsley or rings of green pepper; serve.

Country Beef and Devilled Beef

Cooking time: 2¼ hours
Serves: 4, or 2 for two meals
To store: cover well, to prevent sauce drying, and store in the refrigerator, reheat the next day.

MENU 1
Country Beef with Creamy Potato Topping
Spinach *or* Cabbage
Raisin and Apple Fritters (*page 75*)

MENU 2
Grapefruit
Devilled Beef with Cheese Topping
Peas *or* Beans
Cheese and Biscuits

To freeze: both versions of this stew freeze well.

IMPERIAL	METRIC	AMERICAN
generous 1 lb. chuck steak for stewing	½ kilo chuck steak for stewing	generous 1 lb. shoulder beef for stewing
seasoning	seasoning	seasoning
1 oz. flour	25 g. flour	¼ cup flour
4 tomatoes	4 tomatoes	4 tomatoes
4 carrots	4 carrots	4 carrots
2–3 sticks celery	2–3 sticks celery	2–3 stalks celery
2 oz. fat	50 g. fat	¼ cup shortening
1 pint brown stock *or* water and 1–2 beef stock cubes	½ litre (6 dl.) brown stock *or* water and 1–2 beef stock cubes	2½ cups brown stock *or* water and 1–2 beef bouillon cubes
for topping	*for topping*	*for topping*
3–4 potatoes	3–4 potatoes	3–4 potatoes
1 oz. margarine	25 g. margarine	2 tablespoons margarine
2–3 tablespoons milk	2–3 tablespoons milk	3–4 tablespoons milk

Dice the meat neatly and coat in the seasoned flour. Slice the tomatoes and carrots, chop the celery. Heat the fat in the pan and cook the steak for about 5 minutes, turning once or twice. Gradually work in the stock or water and stock cubes. Bring to the boil and stir over a moderate heat until thickened. Add the prepared vegetables. Lower the heat, cover the pan and cook for nearly 2 hours. Spoon out half the stew for Devilled beef, see below. Continue cooking for about 15 minutes until tender. Meanwhile, cook the potatoes in salted water, strain and mash with half the margarine and the milk. Spoon the stew into a heatproof dish, top with the potatoes and the rest of the margarine and crisp under the grill (broiler).

FOR THE NEXT DAY
Devilled Beef: stir 1–2 teaspoons Worcestershire sauce, 1 tablespoon mustard pickle and a few drops of tomato ketchup (catsup) into remaining stew. Put into an ovenproof casserole, cover with a lid or foil and heat through for approximately 30 minutes in the centre of a moderate oven, 350–375°F (180–190°C), Gas Mark 4–5. Cut 4 slices of French bread, spread one side with butter, sprinkle with a little garlic salt and grated cheese. Remove lid of casserole, put bread rounds on top of the meat, with cheesy-side uppermost, and heat for 15 minutes.

Canned and Frozen Meat Dishes

THESE ARE SOME OF THE CANNED OR
FROZEN MEATS FROM WHICH TO
CHOOSE:

Canned
Corned beef
Frankfurters: to serve instead of
sausages or as an interesting
supper dish
Cooked ham or pork and ham or
bacon grill or similar meats
Cooked tongue (small cans are
generally lamb's tongues)
Stewed kidneys
Stewed steak

Frozen
Chops of various kinds (cook as
fresh)
Hamburgers or similar Meat Cakes
Sausages

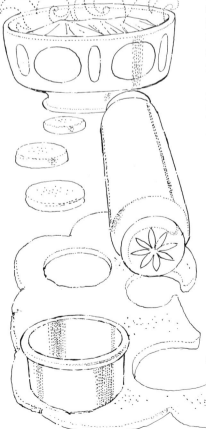

It is always useful to have a few canned meats in the storecupboard from which to produce quick meals, for example:

Corned beef: serve cold, or slice and heat in a little fat; bake in the oven, basting this with a little ginger ale or cider.
Cooked ham or similar meats: slice or dice to serve in salads, or heat in a Tomato sauce, page 24, or a Port wine sauce, page 42, as suggested for tongue.
Tongue: serve cold with salads, or slice and heat in a little butter or stock, or the sauce on page 42.
Stewed kidneys: heat and serve on toast or with vegetables; flavour with a small quantity of red wine.
Stewed steak: heat and serve as a stew; flavour with a little paprika, heat with fresh sliced tomatoes and thinly sliced raw potatoes as a quick *goulash;* or serve as the recipe below. A medium sized can of stewed steak produces one meal for two hungry people, or two lighter meals for two people.

Steak Cobbler: put the stewed steak into a pie dish. Cover with foil and heat for 15 minutes in the centre of a very moderate to moderate oven, 350–375°F (180–190°C), Gas Mark 4–5. Meanwhile, prepare the cobbler mixture: sieve 3 oz. (75 g.–$\frac{3}{4}$ cup) self-raising flour (or plain (all-purpose) flour with 1 level teaspoon baking powder (double acting)) and a pinch salt. Rub in nearly 1 oz. (25 g.–2 tablespoons) margarine, add enough milk to make a soft rolling consistency. Roll out to $\frac{1}{2}$ inch (1 cm.) in thickness. Cut into small rounds, place on top of the meat. Return to the oven, raise the temperature to hot, 425–450°F (220–230°C), Gas Mark 6–7, and bake for 12–15 minutes.

Note. If you make a double amount of the scone topping mixture, bake half the mixture on the meat, as above, then the remainder on a baking tray, you will have scones to serve with cheese or with butter and jam (they are not sweetened, of course).

Shepherd's Pie: put the stewed steak into a pie dish. Top with 1 or 2 sliced tomatoes and very thinly sliced onion or chopped onion. Cover with mashed potato and bake for 30 minutes in the centre of a moderate oven, 375°F (190°C), Gas Mark 5.

Barbecued Frankfurters: heat a small knob of butter in a saucepan, add $\frac{1}{2}$ small can of tomatoes, 1 teaspoon chopped parsley, 1–2 cloves, a pinch mixed herbs, 1 teaspoon sugar and $\frac{1}{2}$ teaspoon Worcestershire sauce. Simmer for a few minutes, then heat 4–6 frankfurters in the sauce, season this well and add a few drops Tabasco sauce.

If you have frankfurters left from a can they can be heated with bacon as a breakfast dish.

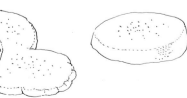

Tongue in Port Wine Sauce

Cooking time: few minutes
Serves: 2
Eat when cooked.

Do *not freeze*.

IMPERIAL	METRIC	AMERICAN
1 orange	1 orange	1 orange
1 tablespoon red-currant jelly	1 tablespoon red-currant jelly	1 tablespoon red currant jelly
wineglass port wine	wineglass port wine	wineglass port wine
4 slices cooked tongue	4 slices cooked tongue	4 slices cooked tongue
seasoning	seasoning	seasoning
pinch sugar	pinch sugar	pinch sugar

Put the orange juice, jelly and port wine into a frying pan or saucepan. Add the tongue and heat gently. Taste and add seasoning; and a pinch of sugar, if wished.

Bean Bake

Cooking time: 45 minutes
Serves: 2
This is better eaten when freshly cooked.

MENU
Bean Bake with Creamed Spinach
Fresh Fruit

Do *not freeze*.

IMPERIAL	METRIC	AMERICAN
small can ham	small can ham	small can ham
1 dessert apple	1 dessert apple	1 dessert apple
1 tablespoon raisins	1 tablespoon raisins	1 tablespoon raisins
small can baked beans	small can baked beans	small can baked beans
1 teaspoon brown sugar	1 teaspoon brown sugar	1 teaspoon brown sugar
1 tablespoon tomato ketchup	1 tablespoon tomato ketchup	1 tablespoon tomato catsup
seasoning	seasoning	seasoning

Dice the meat, peel and dice the apple, then mix all the ingredients together. Put into a casserole, cover and heat for 45 minutes in the centre of a very moderate oven, 325°F (170°C), Gas Mark 3.

To vary
Add chopped chives or grated onion for a more savoury flavour.

Cheese and Beef Bake

Cooking time: 30–35 minutes
Serves: 2
To store: the batter can be made beforehand and kept in a cool place. Serve the dish as soon as it is cooked.

MENU
Cheese and Beef Bake
Blackcurrant Soufflé (*page 74*)

Do *not freeze*.

IMPERIAL	METRIC	AMERICAN
for the batter	*for the batter*	*for the batter*
2 oz. plain flour	50 g. plain flour	½ cup all-purpose flour
pinch salt	pinch salt	pinch salt
1 egg	1 egg	1 egg
¼ pint milk	⅛ litre (1½ dl.) milk	⅔ cup milk
2 oz. grated cheese	50 g. grated cheese	½ cup grated cheese
for the base	*for the base*	*for the base*
3–4 oz. corned beef	75–100 oz. corned beef	3–4 oz. corned beef
2 tomatoes	2 tomatoes	2 tomatoes
½ oz. fat	15 g. fat	1 tablespoon shortening

Sieve the flour and salt. Beat in the egg, milk and cheese. Dice the corned beef and slice the tomatoes. Heat the fat in an ovenproof dish in a really hot to very hot oven, 450–475°F (230–240°C), Gas Mark 7–8. Add the corned beef and tomatoes, return to the oven for 3–4 minutes. Whisk the batter, pour over the corned beef and tomatoes. Return the dish to the top of the oven and bake for approximately 25 minutes. Reduce the temperature slightly after the first 15 minutes.

COOKING CHICKEN AND GAME

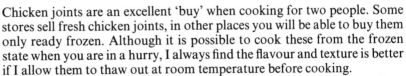

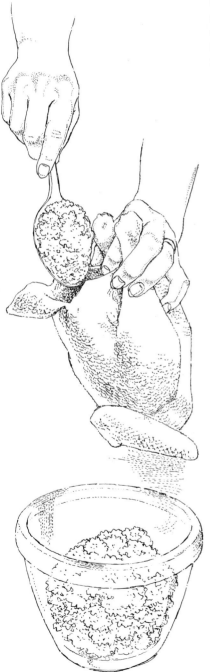

Chicken joints are an excellent 'buy' when cooking for two people. Some stores sell fresh chicken joints, in other places you will be able to buy them only ready frozen. Although it is possible to cook these from the frozen state when you are in a hurry, I always find the flavour and texture is better if I allow them to thaw out at room temperature before cooking.

These chicken joints are very young and tender, so can be grilled (broiled) or fried and used in casserole dishes, added to sauces, etc. Do not over-cook, otherwise the flesh becomes dry and unappetising and lacking in any flavour.

When you want to roast a whole chicken you can choose between small fresh or frozen birds. Always allow a frozen chicken to defrost before roasting it. Page 47 includes suggestions for using cooked chicken, so none of the roast chicken is wasted.

For special occasions you can serve game for two people; pheasant is a 'meaty' game bird and you will find ample on one bird for a hot meal for two, plus some left to serve cold or to heat as suggested for cold chicken. Pigeons and grouse can be used in the same way. Game birds *MUST* be young and tender to roast.

Roast Chicken: stuff if wished, see page 49. Cover the bird with a little dripping, butter, fat bacon or margarine. Roast as meat on page 33, allowing 15 minutes per lb. (weight to include stuffing) and 15 minutes over.

Small roasting chickens can be served with Cranberry or Bread sauce, as pages 48 or 49, or with the same accompaniments as roast game, given at the bottom of this page.

Roast Game: always put a good knob of butter or margarine inside the bird, to make sure it is kept moist, or some people like a knob of cream cheese or a few grapes instead. Cover the bird with plenty of butter or margarine, or with fat bacon, and roast for approximately 45 minutes for the small birds, or 1 hour for a plump pheasant. The temperature is as page 33 for meat.

Accompaniments to serve with game: serve with Bread sauce, page 49, or redcurrant jelly. The traditional garnish is watercress, but lettuce, endive or other green salad can be used instead.

Fry rather coarse breadcrumbs in hot butter until crisp and golden brown, and heat potato crisps (chips) and serve these with the game.

Gravy: make a gravy to serve with roast chicken or game. Simmer the giblets to give a good stock, thicken with a little flour or cornflour (cornstarch), then add some of the fat from the roasting tin.

43

Taunton Chicken

See colour picture page 51

Cooking time: 1 hour
Serves: up to 6
To store: partially cook the day
before required (except the apples)
and keep in the refrigerator;
heat very gently when required.

MENU
Grapefruit and Prawn Cocktail
(*page 8*)
Taunton Chicken with Green Salad
New Potatoes and Peas
Caramel Mousse (*see Note, page 71*)
Cheese and Biscuits

To freeze: frozen chicken joints can
be used for this dish. I do not like this
particular sauce when frozen.

IMPERIAL	METRIC	AMERICAN
either 6 joints of chicken *or* 1 chicken weighing nearly 4½ lb. when trussed	either 6 joints of chicken *or* 1 chicken weighing 2 kilo when trussed	either 6 joints of chicken *or* 1 chicken weighing nearly 4½ lb. when trussed
1 oz. flour	25 g. flour	¼ cup flour
seasoning	seasoning	seasoning
2 oz. butter	50 g. butter	¼ cup butter
1 pint cider	½ litre (6 dl.) cider	2½ cups cider
1 onion	1 onion	1 onion
¼ pint thick cream	⅛ litre (1½ dl.) thick cream	⅔ cup whipping cream
for the garnish	*for the garnish*	*for the garnish*
2–3 dessert apples	2–3 dessert apples	2–3 dessert apples
2 oz. butter	50 g. butter	¼ cup butter
parsley	parsley	parsley
lemon	lemon	lemon

If using frozen chicken, allow the joints to thaw out. If using a whole chicken cut into six joints, i.e. make two joints of each leg, and one joint of each breast and wing. Pull away the skin of the chicken if you want a very smooth coating. Coat the chicken joints in the flour, mixed with the seasoning. Heat the butter in a pan and toss the chicken in this until the outside is very pale golden. Stir in the cider, bring the sauce to the boil and cook gently. Add the whole onion, so the sauce absorbs this flavour during cooking. Simmer for about 45 minutes. Remove the onion and stir in the cream. Cook gently for a few minutes, without boiling. Prepare the garnish while the sauce is cooking: core and slice the apples, but do not peel, and fry gently in the hot butter. Arrange the chicken on a dish and coat with the sauce. Garnish with the apples, parsley and lemon.

To vary
For a thicker sauce, increase the amount of flour slightly.

Use jointed pheasant instead of chicken (this should be enough for 4, not 6 people).

Heat left-over cooked chicken in a similar sauce; use only half the amount of cider, since the sauce will be heated for about 10 minutes only and little of the liquid will evaporate.

Add sliced onion (instead of whole onion), green peas and/or sliced mushrooms to the cider, etc. Naturally these will not be removed when adding the cream, as in the recipe above.

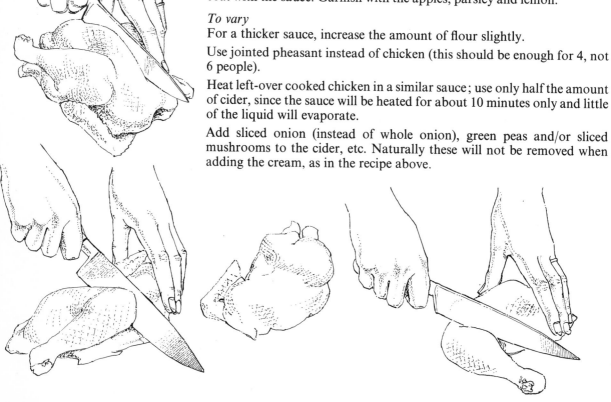

Chicken Rossini

Cooking time: 15 minutes
Serves: 2
Eat as soon as cooked.

MENU
Chicken Rossini
Sauté Potatoes
Green Beans *or* Salad
Cheese and Biscuits

See page 47 for using up the pâté and egg white.

To freeze: fill the chicken with pâté, coat with egg and crumbs, either freeze before *or* after cooking. (Use within 1 month.) Reheat or fry from the frozen state, but see comments on page 43.

IMPERIAL	METRIC	AMERICAN
2 joints breast of chicken	2 joints breast of chicken	2 joints breast of chicken
about 1 oz. liver pâté (half small can)	about 25 g. liver pâté (half small can)	about 1 oz. liver pâté (half small can)
for coating	*for coating*	*for coating*
1 egg yolk	1 egg yolk	1 egg yolk
1 oz. crisp breadcrumbs (raspings)	25 g. crisp breadcrumbs (raspings)	½ cup crisp bread crumbs (raspings)
for frying	*for frying*	*for frying*
2 oz. fat	50 g. fat	¼ cup shortening
to garnish	*to garnish*	*to garnish*
1 tomato	1 tomato	1 tomato

If using frozen chicken, allow to thaw out, then dry thoroughly; wash and dry fresh chicken joints. Make a slit in the flesh to form a 'pocket' and spread with the pâté. Mix the egg yolk with a tablespoon of water, brush the chicken with this. Coat in the crumbs (see sketches below). Heat the fat in the frying pan and fry the chicken quickly on both sides until crisp and brown, then lower the heat and cook gently until tender. Drain on absorbent paper. Top with rings of tomato.

To vary
Chicken Cordon Bleu: use 2 thin slices of ham and 2 thin slices Gruyère or Cheddar cheese instead of pâté. Insert these into the 'pocket' in the chicken.

MORE FILLINGS FOR CHICKEN JOINTS
A filling, such as pâté in the recipe above, or ham and cheese in the variation, not only adds flavour to the chicken, but helps to keep the flesh moist.

Instead of pâté, etc., try a little butter blended with mustard or curry powder, or finely chopped herbs, or with chopped green or red pepper (pimiento).

OTHER INTERESTING FILLINGS WOULD BE
Finely chopped ham or tongue or fried bacon.
Thinly sliced mushrooms, fried in a little butter.

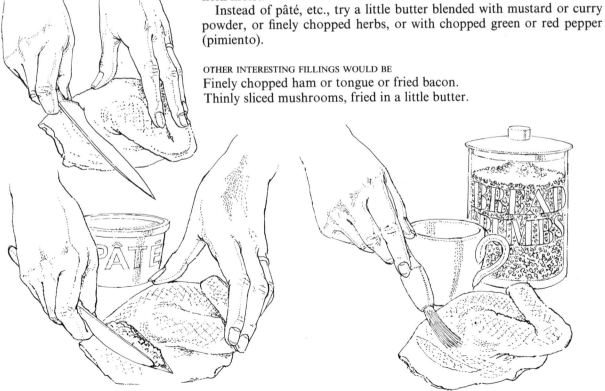

Stuffed Chicken Hotpot

Cooking time: 1½ hours
Serves: 2

To store: serve when cooked, or reheat gently. Keep in the refrigerator for 1 day.

MENU
Cheese Pâté (*page 11*)
Stuffed Chicken Hotpot with Green Vegetable
Baked Apples (*page 67*)

To freeze: the completed dish may be frozen; use within 6 weeks. Frozen chicken joints need defrosting before using.

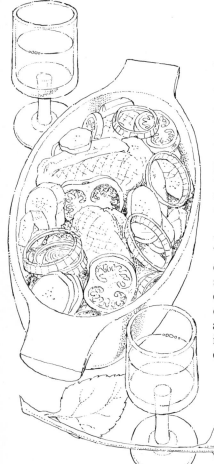

IMPERIAL	METRIC	AMERICAN
2 joints breast of chicken	2 joints breast of chicken	2 joints breast of chicken
for the stuffing and hotpot	*for the stuffing and hotpot*	*for the stuffing and hotpot*
20 oz. calf's *or* lamb's liver*	50 g. calf's *or* lamb's liver*	2 oz. calf's *or* lamb's liver*
1 small and 1 large onion	1 small and 1 large onion	1 small and 1 large onion
1 oz. butter *or* margarine	25 g. butter *or* margarine	2 tablespoons butter *or* margarine
seasoning	seasoning	seasoning
2 large potatoes	2 large potatoes	2 large potatoes
2 large tomatoes	2 large tomatoes	2 large tomatoes
2 tablespoons stock *or* white wine	2 tablespoons stock *or* white wine	2–3 tablespoons stock *or* white wine
pinch dried thyme and rosemary *or* use ¼–½ teaspoon each fresh herbs	pinch dried thyme and rosemary *or* use ¼–½ teaspoon each fresh herbs	pinch dried thyme and rosemary *or* use ¼–½ teaspoon each fresh herbs
for the topping	*for the topping*	*for the topping*
½ oz. butter *or* margarine	15 g. butter *or* margarine	1 tablespoon butter *or* margarine
1 oz. soft coarse breadcrumbs	25 g. soft coarse breadcrumbs	⅓ cup soft coarse bread crumbs

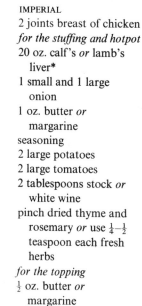

* see page 77 for recipe using rest of the liver if you have bought a larger quantity than given.

If using frozen chicken breasts, allow to thaw out gradually. Meanwhile, chop the liver and small onion very finely, toss in half the butter or margarine, season well. Split each chicken breast to make a 'pocket' and fill with the liver stuffing. Slice the peeled potatoes and large onion thinly and the skinned tomatoes fairly thickly, season. Melt the rest of the butter or margarine, mix with the stock or wine, herbs and seasoning. Put half the potatoes, onion and tomatoes into a deep hotpot; add the chicken breasts and liquid, then cover with sliced tomatoes, onion and finally the potatoes. Cook for about 1¼ hours in the centre of a slow to very moderate oven, 300–325°F (150–170°C), Gas Mark 2–3. Mix the butter or margarine and crumbs together, sprinkle over the top of the potatoes, return to the oven, raise the heat slightly and cook until the crumbs are crisp and brown.

WHEN YOU ENTERTAIN
This is an excellent recipe for a simple party menu. Either buy 4, 6 or 8 chicken joints or a whole young chicken. Cut the latter into joints–if small it will make only 4 joints, 2 breast and wing and 2 legs; if larger you can divide the legs as the recipe on page 44; if very plump then each breast could be divided into 2 portions. If you use a whole jointed chicken, make a slit in the leg joints, remove bones and fill with stuffing. The other ingredients need to be increased according to the number of guests. Increase cooking time by 15 minutes only.

Chicken Croquettes

Cooking time: 8 minutes
Serves: 2
To store: in the refrigerator until
ready to fry.

MENU
Chicken Croquettes with Grilled
(broiled) *or* Fried Tomatoes and
Mushrooms and Salad
Fresh Fruit

To freeze: these freeze excellently.

IMPERIAL	METRIC	AMERICAN
1 good sized cooked chicken portion*	1 good sized cooked chicken portion*	1 good sized cooked chicken portion*
2 oz. soft breadcrumbs	50 g. soft breadcrumbs	⅔ cup soft bread crumbs
3 tablespoons yoghourt	3 tablespoons yoghourt	3–4 tablespoons yogurt
2 teaspoons chopped parsley	2 teaspoons chopped parsley	2 teaspoons chopped parsley
1 egg yolk	1 egg yolk	1 egg yolk
seasoning	seasoning	seasoning
to coat	*to coat*	*to coat*
1 egg white	1 egg white	1 egg white
1 oz. crisp breadcrumbs (raspings)	25 g. crisp breadcrumbs (raspings)	½ cup crisp bread crumbs (raspings)
for frying	*for frying*	*for frying*
2 oz. fat	50 g. fat	¼ cup shortening

* cook an extra chicken portion (when serving fried chicken) for this
purpose; or use about 6 oz. (150 g.) left-over cooked chicken.

Put the chicken through a mincer (use the skin too) or chop very finely.
Blend with the breadcrumbs, yoghourt, parsley, egg yolk and seasoning.
Form into four finger shapes. Brush with the egg white and roll in crisp
breadcrumbs. Fry in hot fat until golden brown. Drain on absorbent
paper. If preferred form into small flat cakes instead of fingers.

To vary
Chicken Pâté Croquettes: use the recipe above, but omit the egg yolk and
add half a can or about 1 oz. (25 g.) pâté. Blend well with the rest of the
ingredients. Form into croquettes, brush with egg white and continue as
the recipe above.

This is an excellent way to use up left-over pâté and a left-over egg white.
Pheasant or other game could be used instead.

If preferred, the mixture may be made into tiny croquettes to serve as
cocktail snacks. Fry, drain and put on to cocktail sticks.

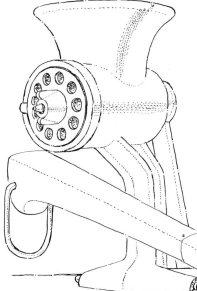

SAUCES AND STUFFINGS

Allow at least ¼ pint (1½ dl.–⅔ cup) of a sauce to serve 2 people, a little more if it is a thickened sauce.

SERVE SAUCES WITH
Fish–choose White Sauce *or* variations on this, *or* Tartare Sauce, *page 50.*

Meat–choose Brown Sauce *or* variations on this, Tomato Sauce, *page 24*, Apple Sauce, *right*, with pork, duck, sausages, etc.

Vegetables–choose White Sauce *or* variations on this.

Poultry–choose Bread Sauce, *page 49*, Cranberry Sauce, *right* (also good with meat), *or* White Sauce *or* variations on this.

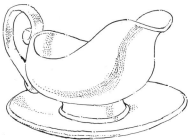

Sauces add interest to so many different dishes and they also help to make a meal more sustaining. When you follow a recipe that normally serves 4 people you will need to make rather more than half quantities for 2 people in order to have sufficient, for whatever amount of cooked sauce you make some is wasted in the pan; so if you make a very small amount you are likely to end up with very little indeed.

I prefer to make a larger quantity of sauce, use the amount needed for 2 servings, cover the remainder with a damp cloth, foil or polythene, and store it for up to 3 days in the refrigerator. Reheat this; add a little extra liquid, and whisk hard to keep it smooth.

Some excellent sauces can be made with dairy soured cream or yoghourt, and this saves using flour, etc., in thickening, for example:

Piquant Sauce: heat a small carton of yoghourt or dairy soured cream (the latter gives a richer sauce) in a basin over hot water. Add 1 tablespoon finely chopped onion or chives, a few drops Worcestershire sauce, ½ teaspoon made-mustard and seasoning.
This sauce blends with vegetables, fish, poultry, veal, etc.
This basic sauce can also be flavoured with curry powder, chopped herbs, grated cheese, soy sauce, tomato ketchup or purée, etc., and all variations of this sauce are very good too when served cold.

Fruit Sauces: the most popular are *Cranberry Sauce* or *Apple Sauce,* but other fruits can be used (*Gooseberry Sauce* is excellent with mackerel or other fish). Simply simmer the fruit with water and sugar until a thick purée. Sieve or emulsify if wished.
A little sherry or port wine can be used in Cranberry sauce.

Cucumber Sauce

No cooking
Serves: 2–4
It would provide rather small portions for 4.
Serve soon after it is made.

MENU
Grilled (broiled) Lamb Cutlets with Cucumber Sauce
Peas, New Potatoes

Do *not freeze.*

IMPERIAL	METRIC	AMERICAN
quarter small cucumber	quarter small cucumber	quarter small cucumber
5 fl. oz. carton (¼ pint) yoghourt	125 g. carton (⅛ litre– 1½ dl.) yoghourt	5 fl. oz. (⅔ cup) yogurt
seasoning	seasoning	seasoning
1 teaspoon chopped parsley	1 teaspoon chopped parsley	1 teaspoon chopped parsley
1 teaspoon chopped chives (*optional*)	1 teaspoon chopped chives (*optional*)	1 teaspoon chopped chives (*optional*)

Peel and cut the cucumber into matchstick pieces, or grate this coarsely. Blend with the rest of the ingredients. This sauce is excellent with curry, fish or meat (lamb in particular).

For a hot sauce: put over a pan of hot water and heat gently–do not boil– stir in a little thick (whipping) cream just before serving.

Bread Sauce

Cooking time: 10 minutes
Serves: 2
To store: covered in a cool place.

To freeze: cover well. This freezes excellently; defrost and reheat. Use within 6–8 weeks.

IMPERIAL	METRIC	AMERICAN
$\frac{3}{8}$ pint (7$\frac{1}{2}$ fl. oz.) milk	2 dl. milk	1 cup milk
1 onion	1 onion	1 onion
1–2 cloves (*optional*)	1–2 cloves (*optional*)	1–2 cloves (*optional*)
about $\frac{1}{2}$ oz. butter	about 15 g. butter	about 1 tablespoon butter
2–3 tablespoons soft breadcrumbs	2–3 tablespoons soft breadcrumbs	3–4 tablespoons soft bread crumbs
seasoning	seasoning	seasoning

Heat the ingredients together, then remove from the heat and leave to infuse in a warm place. Reheat just before serving the meal, stirring well, until the consistency of a thick cream. Remove the onion and cloves before serving.

Note. If you make a larger quantity you can store, then reheat, adding a little cream or milk as you do so.

Rice Stuffing

Cooking time: 50 minutes
Serves: 2, with enough left to make a salad, see below right
To store: covered in a cool place.

MENU
Roast Chicken (*page 43*) with Rice Stuffing
Roast Potatoes
Brussels Sprouts
Whisky Ginger Sundae (*page 66*)

Do *not freeze* the stuffing.

IMPERIAL	METRIC	AMERICAN
1 large *or* 2 small onions	1 large *or* 2 small onions	1 large *or* 2 small onions
1 oz. margarine	25 g. margarine	2 tablespoons margarine
$\frac{3}{4}$ pint good chicken stock* *or* water and 1 chicken stock cube	$\frac{3}{8}$ litre (4$\frac{1}{2}$ dl.) good chicken stock* *or* water and 1 chicken stock cube	2 cups good chicken stock* *or* water and 1 chicken bouillon cube
3 oz. long grain rice	75 g. long grain rice	just under $\frac{1}{2}$ cup long grain rice
seasoning	seasoning	seasoning
few sticks celery	few sticks celery	few stalks celery
$\frac{1}{2}$ green pepper	$\frac{1}{2}$ green pepper	$\frac{1}{2}$ green pepper
1 carrot	1 carrot	1 carrot
1 tablespoon chopped parsley	1 tablespoon chopped parsley	1 tablespoon chopped parsley

* made by simmering giblets.

Chop the onion, toss in the margarine, then add the stock, or water and stock cube, and bring this to the boil. Add the rice, season lightly, then simmer for 10 minutes. Add the diced vegetables and parsley, taste and add extra seasoning. Put into a dish, cover with foil and cook in the coolest part of a moderately hot oven, 400°F (200°C), Gas Mark 5–6, for 30 minutes. If more convenient, finish cooking on top of the cooker, in which case you shorten the cooking time to 15 minutes.

To vary
Add the diced lightly-cooked liver (from the giblets) with celery, etc.
Vegetable Risotto: this is made in the same way as the stuffing. Add to the rice mixture sliced mushrooms (and any other seasonal vegetables) and serve hot.
Rice Salad: blend the cooked rice mixture with a little mayonnaise, some more diced raw celery, the remainder of the green pepper (cut into strips), and 1–2 chopped gherkins. Serve on a bed of lettuce and top with freshly chopped parsley.

Budget Sauces and Stuffings

Sauces are not only a method of making the basic food more interesting, but they save money. A small portion of fish, served with a white or cheese sauce becomes a more nutritious and satisfying meal.

Vegetables, coated with a sauce, can be served as a light main meal without meat, fish or eggs.

In the same way, stuffings help to 'eke out' the more expensive foods, they also help to give flavour and a moist texture to very many different foods—poultry, fish, meat, etc.

The following two sauces are basic ones, capable of infinite variety. I have given the amount often suggested for up to 4 servings, for the reasons outlined on page 48. You can, of course, use half quantities.

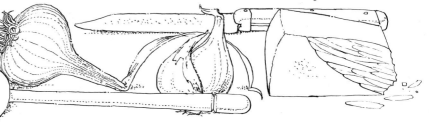

White Sauce

Cooking time: 10 minutes
Serves: up to 4 (depending upon recipe)
To store: see page 48.

To freeze: cover well.

IMPERIAL	METRIC	AMERICAN
1 oz. margarine *or* butter	25 g. margarine *or* butter	2 tablespoons margarine *or* butter
1 oz. flour	25 g. flour	¼ cup flour
½ pint milk	¼ litre (3 dl.) milk	1¼ cups milk
seasoning	seasoning	seasoning

Heat the margarine or butter in a pan, stir in the flour and cook gently for 2–3 minutes, stirring all the time. Gradually add the milk or add it all at once, let it come to the boil and whisk hard rather than stirring continually. Add seasoning.

Flavour white sauce with: anchovy essence, grated cheese (do not boil again after adding the cheese), chopped prawns, parsley, chopped ham (excellent over hard-boiled eggs), etc.

To vary
Brown Sauce: use the method above, but brown stock or water and 1 stock (bouillon) cube.
Flavour brown sauce by using a little more margarine (or fat) and frying chopped onion or other vegetables in this.

Add chopped tomatoes or tomato purée (paste), a little red wine, garlic, or sliced mushrooms to the sauce.

Mayonnaise is essential with many salads. There are excellent commercial makes on the market and they, or a home-made mayonnaise, can be adapted:
Tartare Sauce: add chopped gherkins, parsley and capers to the mayonnaise.
Flavour the mayonnaise with crumbled, sieved or grated cheese (this is an excellent way to use up left-over 'non cooking' cheeses); curry powder; or horseradish cream.

Mayonnaise also can be warmed in a basin over hot water as a hot sauce.

Taunton chicken, see recipe on page 44

EGG DISHES

Eggs can provide some of the quickest and most interesting dishes. The suggestions below and on the following page give some ideas.

Boiled Eggs can be served hot with a white, or cheese, or prawn sauce, or in a curried sauce as below.

Fried Eggs and bacon are an ideal meal when you are in a hurry; the eggs can be made more interesting if topped with a little grated cheese. Fried eggs can be served with fish fingers, hamburgers, sausages, etc.

Poached Eggs are very good on top of creamed spinach, on poached smoked haddock, etc.

Scrambled Eggs are made more satisfying if you add chopped pieces of chicken, ham, flaked fish, grated or crumbled cheese, etc. Since the cooking time is short you can add cheeses such as Camembert, Stilton, etc., that normally are not considered 'cooking cheeses'.

A more savoury version of scrambled egg can be produced if you fry chopped onions, mushrooms, tomatoes, pepper (green or red) in hot butter or margarine before adding the eggs.

Scotch Woodcock: top scrambled egg with anchovy fillets.

Curried Eggs

Cooking time: 20 minutes
Serves: 2
These are better eaten as soon as cooked, as over-cooking spoils the eggs. You can reheat rice, see below, right.

MENU
Avocado Cream (*page 9*)
Curried Eggs with Rice
Fruit Salad and Ice Cream

To freeze: curry sauce freezes well. Hard-boiled eggs cannot be frozen. Rice does not freeze well.

IMPERIAL	METRIC	AMERICAN
3 oz. long grain rice	75 g. long grain rice	just under $\frac{1}{2}$ cup long grain rice
$7\frac{1}{2}$ fl. oz. water	2 dl. water	1 cup water
$\frac{1}{2}$–1 teaspoon salt	$\frac{1}{2}$–1 teaspoon salt	$\frac{1}{2}$–1 teaspoon salt
4 eggs	4 eggs	4 eggs
half quantity Curry sauce, *see page 32*	half quantity Curry sauce, *see page 32*	half quantity Curry sauce, *see page 32*

Boil the rice: the easiest way is to put the rice into cold water and to use about $2\frac{1}{2}$ times the quantity of water to the amount of rice used. Add the salt. Bring the water to the boil, stir briskly; cover the pan, simmer for 15 minutes. If there is any liquid left, remove the lid and let this evaporate over a low heat. Meanwhile, boil the eggs for 6–7 minutes (they will be firmly set, but not too hard). Plunge the eggs into cold water, crack, remove the shells. Put the eggs into the Curry sauce, heat for a few minutes, turning once or twice so they are coated with sauce. Serve with the rice.

TO USE LEFT-OVER RICE
Keep the cooked rice well covered in the refrigerator so it does not dry. Put into cold water to cover. Bring the water to the boil as quickly as possible, strain, then serve.

Omelette

Cooking time: few minutes
Serves: 2
Eat as soon as cooked; the fillings can be prepared beforehand and stored in the refrigerator, or they can be frozen.

Avoid excess washing-up and look after your omelette pan by wiping it out immediately after use.

IMPERIAL	METRIC	AMERICAN
3 or 4 eggs	3 or 4 eggs	3 or 4 eggs
seasoning	seasoning	seasoning
water	water	water
about 1 oz. butter	about 25 g. butter	about 2 tablespoons butter

Beat the eggs lightly with seasoning and a little water. I allow about 1 tablespoon water to each 2 eggs. Heat the butter in the omelette pan, pour in the eggs, leave for a very short time until the egg mixture sets at the bottom of the pan, then tilt the pan, loosening the omelette away from the sides of the pan and continue cooking until lightly set. Fold away from the handle, tip on to a hot dish and serve at once.

The omelette can be filled with grated cheese or crumbled cheese; with hot vegetables; with cooked fish, heated in butter or a little sauce; with cooked ham, chicken, etc.

FOR A MORE AMBITIOUS OMELETTE TRY

Omelette Hongroise: simmer tomatoes with chopped onion, crushed garlic or garlic salt, seasoning and slices of salami. Put into the omelette just before serving.

Omelette Arnold Bennett: blend flaked cooked fish (smoked haddock is particularly good) with the eggs, cook as above. Do not fold the omelette, but slide on to a hot heatproof dish, top with grated cheese, sliced cheese or cheese sauce, and brown under a hot grill (broiler).

Spanish Omelette: fry left-over sliced vegetables, diced ham, prawns, etc., in hot butter until tender. Mix with the beaten eggs. Add a little more butter to the pan, pour in the eggs, cook until firm. Do not fold.

Bretonne Eggs

Cooking time: 20 minutes
Serves: 2
To store: if you want a meal in minutes, prepare the first stage of this dish beforehand, put back into the saucepan, add the eggs and complete cooking.

MENU
Bretonne Eggs with Grilled (broiled) *or* Fried Tomatoes and Watercress
Fresh Fruit and Cheese

IMPERIAL	METRIC	AMERICAN
2 oz. mushrooms	50 g. mushrooms	½ cup mushrooms
1 onion	1 onion	1 onion
2 tablespoons oil	2 tablespoons oil	2–3 tablespoons oil
2 tablespoons long grain rice	2 tablespoons long grain rice	2–3 tablespoons long grain rice
½ pint chicken stock *or* water and 1 chicken stock cube	¼ litre (3 dl.) chicken stock *or* water and 1 chicken stock cube	1¼ cups chicken stock *or* water and 1 chicken bouillon cube
seasoning	seasoning	seasoning
2 oz. prawns *or* mussels *or* flaked fish	50 g. prawns *or* mussels *or* flaked fish	2 oz. prawns *or* mussels *or* flaked fish
few cooked green beans	few cooked green beans	few cooked green beans
3–4 eggs	3–4 eggs	3–4 eggs
little chopped parsley	little chopped parsley	little chopped parsley

Slice the mushrooms and onion fairly finely, toss in the oil with the rice, then add the stock or water and stock cube. Bring to the boil, simmer steadily for about 10 minutes, season well, add the fish and beans and heat for another few minutes. Finally, add the lightly beaten eggs and parsley, and continue cooking until these are set.

CHEESE DISHES

When you consider the variety of cheese you can buy today, your cheese meals always should be interesting. The picture, opposite, shows a simple salad with diced Cheddar (or other hard cheese), grapefruit segments, etc.

Speedy Cheese Soufflé

Cooking time: 15–20 minutes
Serves: 2
Eat as soon as cooked.

MENU
Melon *or* Fruit Juice
Speedy Cheese Soufflé with Creamed Spinach *or* Salad
Ice Cream

Do *not freeze*.

Note. Cheeses to use for soufflés or Welsh rarebit are:
Cheshire or Double Gloucester, Cheddar, Gruyère, Emmenthal, Parmesan, Danish Blue, Dutch cheese

IMPERIAL	METRIC	AMERICAN
4 oz. cheese	100 g. cheese	4 oz. cheese
2 tablespoons thin cream *or* top of the milk	2 tablespoons thin cream *or* top of the milk	2–3 tablespoons coffee cream *or* top of the milk
seasoning	seasoning	seasoning
¾ teaspoon made-mustard	¾ teaspoon made-mustard	¾ teaspoon made-mustard
2–3 eggs	2–3 eggs	2–3 eggs

Blend the finely grated cheese, cream or milk quite briskly, so you make a thick cream-like mixture. Add the seasoning, including the mustard. Separate the eggs and beat the yolks into the cheese mixture, then fold in the stiffly whisked egg whites. Spoon into one or two ovenproof dishes and bake for 15–20 minutes in the centre of a moderate oven, 375°F (190°C), Gas Mark 5. Serve at once.

To vary
Potato Cheese Soufflé: blend equal quantities of mashed potato and grated cheese (about 3 oz. (75 g.) of each). Then add 2 tablespoons thin cream or top of the milk, and seasoning, including a little made-mustard. Separate the yolks from the whites of 2–3 eggs, add the yolks, then fold in the stiffly whisked egg whites. Spoon into the dish or dishes and bake as above, allowing an extra 5 minutes.

Welsh Rarebit

Cooking time: few minutes
Serves: 2
To store: the cheese mixture may be made in a larger quantity, put into a container and stored in the refrigerator for up to 2 weeks. Use as required.

MENU
Welsh Rarebit with Grilled (broiled) Tomatoes
Cake *or* a Light Dessert

IMPERIAL	METRIC	AMERICAN
4–6 oz. cheese	100–150 g. cheese	4–6 oz. cheese
1 oz. butter	25 g. butter	2 tablespoons butter
1 tablespoon beer *or* milk	1 tablespoon beer *or* milk	1 tablespoon beer *or* milk
seasoning	seasoning	seasoning
little made-mustard	little made-mustard	little made-mustard
2 slices toast	2 slices toast	2 slices toast

Mix crumbled or grated cheese with half the butter and other ingredients. Spread on buttered toast and brown under the grill (broiler).

To vary
Buck Rarebit: top the Welsh rarebit with poached or fried eggs. Put mashed sardines, chopped ham or cooked vegetables on the toast, then top with the cheese mixture and grill (broil).

Grapefruit and cheese salad

Savoury Cheese Balls

No cooking
Serves: 2
To store: in a cool place, covered to prevent drying.

MENU
Clear Onion Soup (*page 12*)
Savoury Cheese Balls and Salad
Raisin Fritters (*page 75*)

To freeze: never mix with mayonnaise if you wish to freeze these.
If mixed with milk, use within 2 weeks.

IMPERIAL	METRIC	AMERICAN
4 oz. any type of cheese	100 g. any type of cheese	4 oz. any type of cheese
1–2 gherkins	1–2 gherkins	1–2 gherkins
1–2 olives	1–2 olives	1–2 olives
1 oz. butter	25 g. butter	2 tablespoons butter
1 teaspoon capers	1 teaspoon capers	1 teaspoon capers
2 teaspoons chopped parsley	2 teaspoons chopped parsley	2 teaspoons chopped parsley
seasoning	seasoning	seasoning
little milk *or* mayonnaise	little milk *or* mayonnaise	little milk *or* mayonnaise

Grate hard cheese or mash soft cheese. Chop the gherkins and olives finely; cream the butter. Mix with all the other ingredients, add plenty of seasoning and enough milk or mayonnaise to make a soft rolling consistency. Roll into about six balls and serve with salad.

To vary
Add a grated raw carrot or a little chopped celery.
    Flavour the mixture with a little horseradish cream and/or a few drops of Worcestershire sauce.

For a party: make into balls the size of a hazelnut and roll in crushed potato crisps (chips). Serve on cocktail sticks.

Fondue—an interesting Party Dish

Cooking time: about 20 minutes
Serves: 4–6
Serve when ready.

MENU
Fondue with Toast, Bread, etc., see method

Do *not freeze.*

If you are fortunate enough to have a fondue set you can plan one of the easiest of party menus including a fondue.
    This is made with a cheese that cooks well; and if you want a true Swiss flavour, then use half Emmenthal cheese (the cheese with the large holes) and half Gruyère cheese (this has a similar texture and flavour to Emmenthal but does *NOT* have the holes). A Cheddar cheese, used either by itself or with Gruyère *OR* Emmenthal, is excellent too, and so is a Dutch cheese.
    Do not have the cheese too mature and strong in flavour or dry in texture. If the cheese is very dry it tends to take longer to melt, and this could cause the fondue mixture to separate and become curdled.

IMPERIAL	METRIC	AMERICAN
1 garlic clove (*optional*)	1 garlic clove (*optional*)	1 garlic clove (*optional*)
1 oz. fresh butter	25 g. fresh butter	2 tablespoons fresh butter
8 oz. Gruyère cheese*	200 g. Gruyère cheese*	8 oz. Gruyère cheese*
8 oz. Emmenthal cheese*	200 g. Emmenthal cheese*	8 oz. Emmenthal cheese*
good pinch salt	good pinch salt	good pinch salt
shake pepper	shake pepper	shake pepper
½ pint white wine— choose a dry wine	¼ litre (3 dl.) white wine— choose a dry wine	1¼ cups white wine— choose a dry wine
1 *or* 2 tablespoons brandy (*optional*)	1 *or* 2 tablespoons brandy (*optional*)	1 *or* 2 tablespoons brandy (*optional*)
cornflour (*optional*)— *see method*	cornflour (*optional*)— *see method*	cornstarch (*optional*)— *see method*
to garnish	*to garnish*	*to garnish*
paprika	paprika	paprika

* *or* all Gruyère *or* all Emmenthal *or* all Cheddar cheese.

Cut the clove of garlic in half and rub this round the fondue pan, then remove. Rub the butter round the base and sides of the pan (or the basin if you do not own a fondue set). Grate the cheese fairly finely and put this into the buttered pan with the salt and pepper and most of the wine, together with the brandy.

Cornflour is not essential in a fondue, but if you blend 1 teaspoon cornflour with a little wine and stir this into the cheese mixture as it begins to melt, this helps to prevent the cheese mixture curdling. If you do not wish to use cornflour then pour *all* the wine into the pan with the cheese. Heat the cheese and wine mixture gently, stirring from time to time. Taste when the cheese has melted and add any extra seasoning required. When the cheese is nearly ready either dice French or fresh bread, or cut slices of toast into cubes. Top the fondue with a little paprika and put the bread or toast on plates round the pan. To serve, spear the bread or toast on to fondue or ordinary forks, dip into the hot cheese mixture and eat at once.

To make a change from bread, dip pieces of raw green pepper or tiny cooked mushrooms into the hot cheese, or try large prawns, which I like.

To vary
Beef Fondue: this is the name of the dish in which cubes of fillet or lean rump steak are put on to the fondue forks and left in the hot cheese mixture until sufficiently cooked.

It makes a superb main dish and is one way of making a small quantity of steak 'go further'.

Tomato Fondue: make a fondue as above, but blend either 2–3 tablespoons tomato chutney or 1–2 tablespoons tomato purée (paste) with the cheese mixture. Take particular care that mixture does not curdle.

Vegetable Fondue:–very delicious–add grated raw carrot, shreds of green pepper, tiny button mushrooms and chopped parsley to the cheese mixture when it is hot. Dip the bread dice to coat in the cheese, then spear tiny pieces of vegetable on too.

Made in minute Fondues

Serve as a first course or a party dish.

Cheese Sauce Fondue: make a Cheese sauce as page 50, but use a little less liquid so the sauce is thicker, season well and keep hot.

Tomato and Cheese Fondue: heat a small can of condensed (concentrated) tomato soup, flavour this with grated Cheddar, Gruyère or other cooking cheese.

Other canned soups can be used as the basis for a fondue or 'dip', the most suitable being a thick cream of asparagus soup; a bisque of shrimp or other shellfish; a cream of mushroom soup.

Do not let the mixture become too hot after adding the cheese.

PASTRY DISHES

If you are short of time you can buy very good frozen or packet pastry mixes, but a short crust pastry is really very simple to make. This is the most versatile of all pastries, for you can use it for sweet and savoury dishes, for pies, tarts, etc. A few suggestions are given below. I have given a quantity that would make enough for 1 small flan, but you may prefer to make a larger quantity and store this. When using the pastry for sweet flans, etc., add 2–3 teaspoons sugar.

Short Crust Pastry

Cooking time: about 20 minutes
Serves: 2 generous portions, or up to 4 small portions

Savoury flans and quiche can be served as a light meal, or they are excellent as part of the menu for a buffet party.
Serve a Quiche Lorraine as an hors d'oeuvre.

To freeze: pastry and Quiche Lorraine freeze well, but you will need to use at least 50 per cent cream in the filling of the quiche.

IMPERIAL	METRIC	AMERICAN
4 oz. plain flour	100 g. plain flour	1 cup all-purpose flour
pinch salt	pinch salt	pinch salt
2 oz. margarine, butter *or* fat	50 g. margarine, butter *or* fat	$\frac{1}{4}$ cup margarine, butter *or* shortening
water to mix	water to mix	water to mix

Sieve the flour and salt. Rub in the margarine, butter or fat until the mixture looks like fine breadcrumbs. Bind with water (you will need about 1 tablespoon). Roll out and line a 6-inch (15-cm.) flan ring on an upturned baking tray, or a flan dish. Fill with greased greaseproof paper (greased-side touching the pastry) and with haricot (navy) beans or crusts of bread. Bake 'blind' for 15 minutes in the centre of a hot oven, 425–450°F (220–230°C), Gas Mark 6–7, then remove the paper, etc., and the flan ring, and continue cooking until golden and firm.

SAVOURY FILLINGS
Make a White sauce as page 50, but use only $7\frac{1}{2}$ fl. oz. (2 dl.–1 cup) milk. Add to the sauce diced ham, grated cheese, cooked sliced mushrooms or other vegetables. Put into the pastry.

Quiche Lorraine: bake the pastry as above for 15 minutes only. Remove from the oven. Blend 2 eggs with $7\frac{1}{2}$ fl. oz. (2 dl.–1 cup) milk, 3–4 oz. (75–100 g.–$\frac{3}{4}$–1 cup) grated cheese, seasoning and a little chopped cooked bacon. Pour into the pastry case, return to the oven–lowering the heat to very moderate–and set for about 40 minutes.

SWEET FILLINGS
Fill the pastry with ice cream and a sauce, see suggestions on page 66.

Fill the cooked and cooled flan with well drained fruit. Blend 1 teaspoon arrowroot with about $\frac{1}{4}$ pint ($1\frac{1}{2}$ dl.–$\frac{2}{3}$ cup) fruit syrup from the can or from cooking the fruit. Pour into a saucepan; add a little sugar or lemon juice, or a tablespoon redcurrant jelly, for extra flavour. Bring slowly to the boil, stir well and heat gently until thickened. Spoon over the fruit when cooled.

Strawberry roll Chantilly, see recipe on page 73

VEGETABLES AND SALADS

On these pages are some very interesting and pleasant ways to serve vegetables, including light main dishes.

Beetroot: this makes an excellent hot vegetable. Grate or dice the cooked beetroot and mix with hot margarine, or blend with white or cheese sauce, page 50. Hot beetroot is particularly good with fish.

Cabbage: if you are tired of cooked cabbage, use any left in a salad. Shred the cabbage finely, mix with mayonnaise, nuts, raisins, grated apple, chopped celery, etc.

Courgettes: these are ideal for a small family, for you can buy several only. They can be cooked in a very little stock or water with plenty of seasoning, or in 2–3 tablespoons water or stock and a good knob of fat, or they can be sliced, coated with seasoned flour and fried, as opposite. Do not peel courgettes (often called small zucchini), remove the ends and slice fairly thinly or halve lengthways.

Cucumber: it is not easy to buy less than half a cucumber; if some is left from a salad use this in a soup or sauce (pages 12 and 48) or as a hot vegetable. Slice the cucumber thinly, dip in seasoned flour and fry, as opposite; or simmer in salted water for about 8 minutes, drain, toss in butter and chopped parsley. The cucumber is better peeled if the skin is tough.

Tomatoes: use as the sauce on page 24, or add to stews and casseroles. One of the best hors d'oeuvre is a *Tomato Salad* made by slicing firm tomatoes, turning the slices in blended oil, vinegar, seasoning, chopped chives and/or basil. Season well; arrange on shredded lettuce.

Soufflé Jacket Potatoes

Cooking time: from 1 hour
Serves: 2
Serve as soon as the potatoes are cooked.

MENU
Bacon *or* Sausages with
Soufflé Jacket Potatoes
Baked Apples (*page 67*) and Cream

Do *not* freeze.

IMPERIAL	METRIC	AMERICAN
2 medium sized old potatoes	2 medium sized old potatoes	2 medium sized old potatoes
1 oz. margarine	25 g. margarine	2 tablespoons margarine
seasoning	seasoning	seasoning
2 eggs	2 eggs	2 eggs
1 tablespoon milk	1 tablespoon milk	1 tablespoon milk
2 oz. grated Cheddar *or* Gruyère cheese	50 g. grated Cheddar *or* Gruyère cheese	½ cup grated Cheddar *or* Gruyère cheese
1 egg white (*optional*)	1 egg white (*optional*)	1 egg white (*optional*)

Bake the potatoes in their jackets for about 1 hour, temperature as below. Split through the centre, remove the pulp into a basin and mash with the margarine and seasoning. Separate the egg yolks from the whites and beat the yolks, milk and cheese into the potato mixture. Whip the egg whites stiffly, fold into the potato purée. Spoon into the potato skins and bake for 15 minutes in the centre of a moderately hot oven, 375–400°F (190–200°C), Gas Mark 5–6.

60

Some Fried Vegetables

Cooking time: about 8 minutes
To store: keep cooked or raw vegetables in as cool a place as possible.

To freeze: always check in your instruction book before freezing vegetables.

The cover picture shows one of the most pleasant of fried vegetables, i.e. *courgettes*. Slice the unpeeled vegetables, coat in a little seasoned flour and fry steadily in hot fat or oil until tender, turn during cooking until golden brown on both sides.

Aubergines (*eggplants*) can be fried in just the same way—slice thinly.
Sauté Potatoes: for this recipe the potatoes need to be cooked until just tender, but unbroken. Slice fairly thickly and fry in hot fat until golden brown on both sides, top with chopped parsley.

Fried Potatoes: peel the potatoes and cut into slices or chip shapes (French fries). Dry well before cooking. Heat fat or oil in the pan and cook the potatoes until tender, but not brown. Lift out of the pan, reheat the fat or oil then fry the potatoes for 2 minutes, or until very brown and crisp. Drain on absorbent paper.

Casserole of Aubergines and Tomatoes

Cooking time: 1 hour
Serves: 2 as a main dish, or 4 with fish, meat, etc.
To store: can be kept and reheated.

MENU
Fish Pâté (*page 10*)
Casserole of Aubergines and Tomatoes
Green Salad
Fruit and Cream

To freeze: freezes well after cooking. Can be kept for some months before using.

IMPERIAL	METRIC	AMERICAN
2 medium sized aubergines	2 medium sized aubergines	2 medium sized eggplants
1 oz. margarine *or* butter	25 g. margarine *or* butter	2 tablespoons margarine *or* butter
seasoning	seasoning	seasoning
chopped chives *or* onions to taste	chopped chives *or* onions to taste	chopped chives *or* onions to taste
8 oz. tomatoes	200 g. tomatoes	8 oz. tomatoes
1 tablespoon water *or* white wine	1 tablespoon water *or* white wine	1 tablespoon water *or* white wine
for the topping	*for the topping*	*for the topping*
1 oz. soft breadcrumbs	25 g. soft breadcrumbs	$\frac{1}{3}$ cup soft bread crumbs
1 oz. grated Cheddar *or* Gruyère cheese	25 g. grated Cheddar *or* Gruyère cheese	$\frac{1}{4}$ cup grated Cheddar *or* Gruyère cheese

Wash, dry, but do not peel the aubergines, slice thinly. If you dislike the slightly bitter taste of the skins, score the skins *before* slicing, sprinkle lightly with salt, leave for about 20 minutes, *then* slice. Toss in the melted margarine or butter, season and flavour with the chives or onions. Skin and slice the tomatoes, put alternate layers of aubergines and seasoned tomatoes into a shallow casserole, end with tomatoes; add water or wine. Cover with a lid, bake for about 45 minutes in the centre of a very moderate to moderate oven, 350–375°F (180–190°C), Gas Mark 4–5, then top with the crumbs, blended with the cheese and continue cooking for a further 10–15 minutes. If wished, omit the topping and cover the tomatoes with a little margarine then a lid or buttered foil, and cook for nearly 1 hour.

To vary
Use thinly-sliced onions and tomatoes; excellent with hot or cold meats.

Use thickly-sliced potatoes and thinly-sliced onions; ideal to serve with cold or hot meat when you do not wish to have gravy or sauce, for the potatoes are very moist. Sliced tomatoes could also be added, if wished.

Mushroom and Cauliflower Mornay

Cooking time: 25 minutes
Serves: 2 as a main dish, 4 as an hors d'oeuvre
Serve as soon as cooked.

MENU
Grapefruit
Mushroom and Cauliflower Mornay
New Potatoes

Do *not freeze.*

IMPERIAL	METRIC	AMERICAN
1 small cauliflower	1 small cauliflower	1 small cauliflower
seasoning	seasoning	seasoning
2 oz. mushrooms	50 g. mushrooms	½ cup mushrooms
2 oz. butter *or* margarine	50 g. butter *or* margarine	¼ cup butter *or* margarine
1 oz. flour	25 g. flour	¼ cup flour
½ pint milk	¼ litre (3 dl.) milk	1¼ cups milk
4 oz. grated Cheddar *or* Gruyère cheese	100 g. grated Cheddar *or* Gruyère cheese	1 cup grated Cheddar *or* Gruyère cheese

Prepare the cauliflower by removing any tough green stalks, but leave it whole. Put into boiling salted water and cook until *JUST* tender; do not over-cook. Meanwhile, slice the mushrooms and heat in half the butter or margarine for 2–3 minutes. Lift out of the saucepan and put into a basin. Blend the flour with just over half the milk, pour into the saucepan, add the rest of the butter or margarine and cook until a thick mixture. Season well. Lift the cauliflower from the water. Drain and put into a dish, cut out the centre (see the picture). Chop and mix this with the mushrooms, *half* the thick sauce and *half* the cheese. Pile this back into the centre of the cauliflower, put into the oven (set to very moderate to keep hot). Blend the rest of the milk into the remaining thick sauce, whisk sharply until smooth. Heat, add the rest of the cheese and any extra seasoning required. Pour over the cauliflower and serve.

Stuffed Onions

Cooking time: 1¼ hours
Serves: 2
This dish is better served as soon as it is cooked.

MENU
Orange Juice
Stuffed Onions with Jacket Potatoes (bake for 1–1½ hours, temperature as in method)
Baked Apples filled with Mixed Dried Fruit (*page 67*)

Do *not freeze.*

IMPERIAL	METRIC	AMERICAN
seasoning	seasoning	seasoning
2 large onions	2 large onions	2 large onions
4 oz. cooked *or* canned meat	100 g. cooked *or* canned meat	4 oz. cooked *or* canned meat
2 oz. Cheddar *or* Gruyère cheese	50 g. Cheddar *or* Gruyère cheese	2 oz. Cheddar *or* Gruyère cheese
pinch mixed herbs	pinch mixed herbs	pinch mixed herbs
1 egg	1 egg	1 egg
1 tablespoon soft breadcrumbs	1 tablespoon soft breadcrumbs	1 tablespoon soft bread crumbs
½ oz. butter	15 g. butter	1 tablespoon butter
small can tomatoes	small can tomatoes	small can tomatoes

Half fill a pan with water, season well. Put in the peeled onions, cover the pan and simmer steadily for about 25 minutes. Lift the onions from the liquid. Cool slightly, remove the centres of the onions, chop finely. Put into a basin and mix with the finely chopped cooked or canned meat (corned beef, luncheon meat, etc.), grated or diced cheese, herbs, egg and crumbs. Season well. Put the onion 'shells' into an ovenproof dish and press the stuffing into the centres. Top with the butter. Pour the tomatoes round the onions, sprinkle with seasoning. Cover the dish with a lid or foil, and cook for 50 minutes in a very moderate to moderate oven, 350–375°F (180–190°C), Gas Mark 4–5.
Pieces of chopped left-over meat could be added to the stuffing.

Orange and sultana syllabub, see recipe on page 72

Salads
for Two

No cooking
To store: arrange the salad, cover with foil or polythene and keep in a cool place.

French Dressing for a salad is made by blending oil, vinegar or lemon juice with seasoning and a pinch of sugar.
Add chopped fresh herbs.
Store in a screw-topped jar.

It is a good idea to specialise in interesting salads that use few ingredients.
Avocado, Onion and Tomato: peel, halve and slice an avocado pear, toss in oil and vinegar, then blend with 1 thinly sliced raw onion and 1–2 sliced tomatoes. (Orange segments could be used instead of onion.)
    This salad is delicious as an hors d'oeuvre, or with cold meat or poultry. It would then serve 4.

Pepper and Tomato: cut rings of red and green pepper (pimiento) discard the seeds; arrange on lettuce and sliced tomato.

Stuffed Ham Rolls: blend diced cooked or canned potatoes, diced celery, chopped gherkin with mustard-flavoured mayonnaise. Put on slices of cooked ham. Serve with mixed salad. Picture page 23.

Salad
Parmentier

Cooking time: 10 minutes
Serves: 2
To store: wrap in foil and keep in the refrigerator for a few hours.

MENU
This is a meal in itself. Serve with Rolls *or* Bread and Butter and Fresh Fruit.

Do *not freeze.*

IMPERIAL	METRIC	AMERICAN
2 eggs	2 eggs	2 eggs
6 oz. cooked new potatoes	150 g. cooked new potatoes	6 oz. cooked new potatoes
4 oz. Cheddar cheese	100 g. Cheddar cheese	4 oz. Cheddar cheese
2 oz. cooked ham	50 g. cooked ham	2 oz. cooked ham
3 tablespoons mayonnaise	3 tablespoons mayonnaise	3–4 tablespoons mayonnaise
1 tablespoon top of the milk	1 tablespoon top of the milk	1 tablespoon top of the milk
2 teaspoons lemon juice	2 teaspoons lemon juice	2 teaspoons lemon juice
lettuce	lettuce	lettuce

Hard boil the eggs, then put them in cold water; remove the shells. Dice the eggs, potatoes, cheese and ham. Blend the mayonnaise, milk and lemon juice, then mix with the potatoes, etc. Spoon on to a bed of lettuce.

Citrus
Petal Salad

No cooking
Serves: 2 or 3
To store: arrange on the dish, cover with foil and keep in the refrigerator.

MENU
Cold Chicken *or* Game *or* Meat *or* Hot Trout with Citrus Petal Salad Cheese and Biscuits

Do *not freeze.*

IMPERIAL	METRIC	AMERICAN
½ grapefruit*	½ grapefruit*	½ grapefruit*
1 orange	1 orange	1 orange
1 tangerine	1 tangerine	1 tangerine
few lettuce leaves	few lettuce leaves	few lettuce leaves
1 dessert apple	1 dessert apple	1 dessert apple
French dressing, *above, left*	French dressing, *above, left*	French dressing, *above, left*
few nuts (any variety)	few nuts (any variety)	few nuts (any variety)

* use the rest in a Grapefruit cocktail (*page 8*).

Cut the skin from the grapefruit and orange; this means you remove the outer pith as you do so. Divide the fruit into neat segments, discarding skin and pips. Peel the tangerine and divide into segments. Put the lettuce leaves on to a flat dish, arrange the fruit like the petals of a flower. Dice the apple (discard the core but do not peel). Coat in the dressing so it does not discolour, add the nuts and then spoon into the centre of the 'petals'.

RICE AND PASTA

Both rice and pasta have similar advantages – they can be cooked in small quantities; they blend with almost all savoury ingredients; they provide the basis of a good meal in a short time.

Choose long grain rice for savoury dishes, not the round or short grain (Carolina) rice, which is normally used for puddings.

Look around shops and stores and see the very large variety of pasta shapes. Spaghetti is given below, but the other shapes could be used instead.

Fortunately both rice and pasta do not deteriorate in packet form, so you can keep good stocks in the house.

Creamy Rice Ring: cook the long grain rice in salted water, add a small packet of frozen vegetables to the rice, etc. Make a Cheese sauce as page 50, and when thickened blend in a little left-over cooked fish. Form the rice and vegetable mixture into a ring, fill with the cheese mixture.

Curried Rice: fry 1 sliced onion in a little margarine. Add 1–2 teaspoons curry powder. Add the rice, water and salt, bring to the boil and cook until soft. Add diced cooked meat, a few sultanas and a sprinkling of desiccated (shredded) coconut. Spoon on to a hot dish and top with chopped hard-boiled egg.

Flaked cooked fish could be used in place of meat.

Cheddar Rice: cook the rice until tender, then add grated cheese and diced tomato to the rice, heat for 2–3 minutes and serve.

Quick ideas with rice

If you allow 3 oz. (75 g. – $\frac{1}{2}$ cup) rice and $7\frac{1}{2}$ fl. oz. (2 dl. – 1 cup) water and salt to taste, you have sufficient for 2 reasonable servings.

Put the rice into cold salted water, bring to the boil, stir briskly. Cover the pan, lower the heat, simmer for 15 minutes.

Quick ideas with spaghetti

If you allow 4 oz. (100 g.) pasta for 2 people you have sufficient for 2 reasonable servings.

Put the pasta into 2 pints (generous litre – good 5 cups) boiling salted water, cook until just tender, then strain.

Spaghetti alla Carbonara (spaghetti with bacon and egg): cook the spaghetti. Meanwhile, chop and fry 3 rashers (slices) of bacon in a large saucepan. When crisp, add 2 tablespoons thin cream or top of the milk, a little chopped parsley and 2–3 beaten eggs – do not cook again when the eggs are added. Strain the spaghetti, tip into the bacon mixture, add seasoning and a little grated cheese and heat for 1–2 minutes. Serve at once with more cheese.

Spaghetti alla Marinara (spaghetti with fish). This is an excellent recipe to 'use up' small quantities of fish remaining, anchovies left over from another dish, etc. Cook the spaghetti. Meanwhile, fry 1 chopped onion and/or a few sliced mushrooms plus 2 large sliced tomatoes in a little margarine or butter. Add a very little water (or use half a can of tomatoes with some of the liquid). Add the chopped cooked fish (any kind) and a little seasoning. Strain the spaghetti, tip into the fish mixture, heat for a few minutes, add seasoning, a little chopped parsley and/or lemon juice. Serve with more cooked tomatoes and/or grated cheese.

DESSERTS

One of the best desserts for any sized family is to end the meal with raw fruit. Many fruits, the citrus ones in particular, are an excellent source of vitamin C, and this is lost during cooking.

Some fruits, of course, are better when cooked, and this is where you can save yourself time if you cook a rather larger amount than you need for one meal, then use the remainder in an entirely different dish.

TO COOK FRUIT, SO THAT IT LOOKS ATTRACTIVE AND THE FRUIT REMAINS WHOLE OR IN GOOD SHAPE

Boil a little sugar or honey and water to form a syrup. Put in the prepared fruit and simmer gently until tender.

Very soft fruits, such as blackcurrants, etc., can be cooked by adding them to the hot syrup, covering the pan at once and leaving it off the cooker. The steam from the syrup cooks the fruit without it breaking and forming a pulp. Serve as a *Compote of Fruit*.

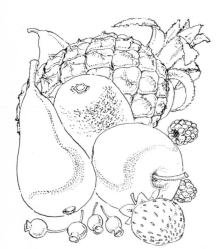

Ways to use cooked fruit

All suggestions serve 2
To store: in a cool place.

ANY FRUIT LEFT-OVER CAN BE USED FOR

1 A sauce to serve over ice cream; sieve or emulsify the fruit, if wished.
2 *Fruit Snow:* strain off the surplus liquid, sieve, mash or emulsify the fruit. To ½ pint (3 dl.–1¼ cups) fruit pulp allow 2 egg whites stiffly whisked with a little extra sugar. Fold the egg whites into the fruit, pile into glasses and chill.
3 *Fruit Cobbler:* put the fruit into a pie dish. Make the cobbler mixture as page 41, but add a tablespoon sugar to the flour, etc. Heat the fruit for a short time, put the rounds of scone mixture on top and continue cooking as page 41.

Ice Cream Desserts

To store: keep the ice cream in the freezing compartment.
Make the sauces in larger quantities, store in covered containers in the refrigerator, use or heat as required for sundaes, etc.

Ice cream has become such a popular dessert that one needs to 'ring the changes'; try some of these sauces:

Chocolate Sauce: either melt about 3 oz. (75 g.) plain (unsweetened) chocolate in a basin over hot water *or* heat a good ½ oz. (15 g.–1 tablespoon) butter, 2 tablespoons water, 1 tablespoon golden (light corn) syrup, 1 tablespoon sugar and 1 tablespoon cocoa until a smooth sauce. (American spoon measures should be increased slightly.)
Mocha Sauce: follow the recipe for Chocolate sauce, but use a strong coffee instead of water.
Caramel Sauce: use some of the Caramel sauce on page 69, heating this or diluting it with a little cream for a cold sauce.
Whisky Ginger Sauce: make a syrup of 4 tablespoons orange juice and 2 tablespoons sugar, add 2 tablespoons whisky and a little chopped ginger.

Baked Apples

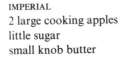

Cooking time: see method
Serves: 2
To store: although many people like
a cold baked apple, it is probably
easier to remove the skins from the
fruit before storing and mash the
pulp, ready to make another dish.

MENU
Baked Apples would be an excellent
dessert for many meals where the
oven is in use for the main dish.

Do *not freeze.*

IMPERIAL	METRIC	AMERICAN
2 large cooking apples	2 large cooking apples	2 large baking apples
little sugar	little sugar	little sugar
small knob butter	small knob butter	small knob butter

Core the apples and slit the skins round the middle, so the pulp will not break through. Stand in an ovenproof dish and fill the centres with sugar and top with a little butter. If you like a certain amount of juice with the fruit, put 2–3 tablespoons water in the dish. The baking time naturally varies with the size of the apples, but you can also adapt this according to the rest of the menu.

Allow 50 minutes to 1 hour in a moderately hot oven (a hotter oven is not good as the outside of the fruit becomes soft before the inside is cooked); 1–1¼ hours in a moderate oven or 1¼–1½ hours in a slow oven.

It is worthwhile cooking extra apples, removing the skins while hot, then using them as apple sauce or in a dessert, see left and below, also page 66.

To vary
Fill the apples with golden (light corn) syrup, mixed dried fruit, bramble jelly, or crushed blackberries and sugar, etc.

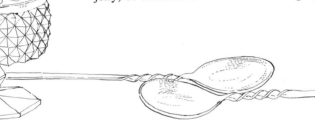

Apple Ginger Creams

Cooking time: see method, *above, right.*
Serves: 2
To store: in a cool place for 1–2 days.

MENU
Spaghetti alla Marinara (*page 65*)
with Salad
Apple Ginger Creams

To freeze: freezes well. Keep for 4–5 months, but do not add cream until serving.

IMPERIAL	METRIC	AMERICAN
2 baked apples, *see above*	2 baked apples, *see above*	2 baked apples, *see above*
2 ginger nut biscuits	2 ginger nut biscuits	2 ginger snap cookies
1 oz. crystallised ginger	25 g. crystallised ginger	1 oz. candied ginger
1–2 oz. sugar	25–50 g. sugar	⅛–¼ cup sugar
few drops green colouring (*optional*)	few drops green colouring (*optional*)	few drops green coloring (*optional*)
to decorate	to decorate	to decorate
4 tablespoons thick *or* thin cream	4 tablespoons thick *or* thin cream	5 tablespoons whipping *or* coffee cream

Remove the skins from the apples while still hot. Take all the pulp from the fruit and put into a basin. Discard the cores. Leave until cold. Break the ginger nut biscuits into tiny pieces and slice the crystallised ginger, save several small pieces for decoration. Blend the ginger nut crumbs, sliced ginger and sugar into the apple pulp and tint a pale green. Spoon into two glasses and pour the cream over the top. Decorate with the tiny pieces of ginger just before serving.

To vary
Try this recipe using plain sweet biscuits (cookies) instead of ginger nuts, and flavour with the grated rind of a lemon or orange and a generous tablespoon lemon or orange marmalade.

Mashed or sieved cooked or canned rhubarb can be used instead of apples in the recipe above. Do not use any of the rhubarb syrup, for this would give too soft a mixture.

Orange and Wine Compote

Cooking time: 10 minutes
Serves: 2
To store: for 1–2 days in the refrigerator.

MENU
Creamy Rice Ring (*page 65*)
Orange and Wine Compote

To freeze: keeps well in the freezer for 2–3 months.

IMPERIAL	METRIC	AMERICAN
4 oranges, preferably seedless	4 oranges, preferably seedless	4 oranges, preferably seedless
¼ pint water	⅛ litre (1½ dl.) water	⅔ cup water
¼ pint red wine	⅛ litre (1½ dl.) red wine	⅔ cup red wine
2 oz. sugar	50 g. sugar	¼ cup sugar
¼ teaspoon ground ginger	¼ teaspoon ground ginger	¼ teaspoon ground ginger
½ teaspoon ground cinnamon	½ teaspoon ground cinnamon	½ teaspoon ground cinnamon

Cut the top 'zest' from the oranges, do not use any white pith. Put the 'zest' into the saucepan with the water, wine, sugar and spices. Simmer for 10 minutes in a *covered* saucepan. Meanwhile, cut away the pith from the fruit then slice neatly. Arrange the oranges in a dish. Strain the wine liquid over the fruit. Serve hot or cold with cream or ice cream.

To vary
Tangerines are equally delicious served this way.

Yoghourt Fool

Cooking time: see method
Serves: 2
To store: for 1–2 days in the refrigerator.

MENU
Fresh Tomato Salad (*page 60*)
Seafood Risotto (*page 17*)
Yoghourt Fool

To freeze: cover well and use within 6–8 weeks.

IMPERIAL	METRIC	AMERICAN
¼ pint fruit purée (*see method*)	⅛ litre (1½ dl.) fruit purée (*see method*)	⅔ cup fruit purée (*see method*)
¼ pint yoghourt	⅛ litre (1½ dl.) yoghourt	⅔ cup yogurt
sugar to taste	sugar to taste	sugar to taste
to decorate	*to decorate*	*to decorate*
few halved walnuts *or* other nuts	few halved walnuts *or* other nuts	few halved walnuts *or* other nuts
whole fruit	whole fruit	whole fruit

To make the fruit purée, sieve or emulsify raw soft berry fruits or cooked hard fruits, pour off any surplus juice before doing this. Cook apples, plums, etc., with the minimum of water to give a thick purée. Blend the cold purée, yoghourt and sugar. Spoon into sundae glasses and top with nuts and/or whole fruit. Chill well.

Melon Cream

No cooking–*freeze* for a short time if possible.
Serves: up to 4

MENU
This makes a delicious dessert for any special menu.

This is an ideal way of using part of a melon. The proportions assume you are using half a medium sized melon. Remove the seeds, then the pulp. Sieve, mash or emulsify this until smooth. Blend with 7½ fl. oz. (2 dl.– 1 cup) thick lightly-whipped cream, a little sugar, lemon juice to flavour. Colour a delicate green with 2–3 drops colouring. Spoon back into the melon skin or into a dish. Although this can be served chilled, it is even nicer if lightly frozen.

Caramel Sauce

Cooking time: about 10 minutes
Serves: 8, or use in 4 recipes, see this page and pages 71 and 74
To store: in a screw-topped jar.

To freeze: pointless to freeze this sauce as it keeps so well.

IMPERIAL	METRIC	AMERICAN
10 oz. loaf, granulated *or* castor sugar	generous 250 g. loaf, granulated *or* castor sugar	1¼ cups lump *or* granulated sugar
½ pint water	¼ litre (3 dl.) water	1¼ cups water

This sauce is an excellent 'stand-by', so make this quantity and use as required.

Put the sugar and half the water into a strong saucepan. Stir over a medium heat until the sugar dissolves, then boil steadily, *WITHOUT STIRRING,* until a golden brown caramel. Add the rest of the water and heat until a smooth sauce. Cool slightly (so you do not crack the jar) then pour into the container.

Note. The Caramel sauce may stiffen slightly with storage, but it can always be diluted with a little warm water or warm milk.

Golden syrup (or half light corn or maple syrup and half sugar) instead of all sugar and water, may be heated to make a caramel.

Caramelled Apples and Oranges

No cooking
Serves: 2
To store: in a cool place for a few hours only.

Do not freeze.

IMPERIAL	METRIC	AMERICAN
2 small *or* 1 large orange	2 small *or* 1 large orange	2 small *or* 1 large orange
2 small dessert apples	2 small dessert apples	2 small dessert apples
a quarter of the Caramel sauce, *above*	a quarter of the Caramel sauce, *above*	a quarter of the Caramel sauce, *above*

Cut the peel from the oranges, then slice the fruit thinly. Peel and core the apples and cut into rings. Arrange fruit in a dish or two glasses. Add the Caramel sauce. Leave standing for 1 hour if possible.

To vary
Honey Apples and Oranges: use honey in place of Caramel sauce.

Ice Cream Medley: dice the fruit rather than slice. Mix with the Caramel sauce. Spoon over ice cream.

Caramelled Banana Slices

Cooking time: 8 minutes
Serves: 2
Serve as soon as possible after cooking.

MENU
Liver Pâté (*page 10*)
Hotpot Portuguese (*page 18*) with Creamed Spinach
Caramelled Banana Slices

To freeze: banana dishes do not freeze very well, except where the bananas are mashed, as in ice cream.

IMPERIAL	METRIC	AMERICAN
2 sponge cakes (type used for trifles)	2 sponge cakes (type used for trifles)	2 sponge cakes (type used for trifles)
1½ oz. butter *or* margarine	40 g. butter *or* margarine	3 tablespoons butter *or* margarine
apricot jam	apricot jam	apricot jam
4 small *or* 2 large bananas	4 small *or* 2 large bananas	4 small *or* 2 large bananas
2–3 tablespoons brown sugar	2–3 tablespoons brown sugar	3–4 tablespoons brown sugar

Split the sponge cakes. Fry in the hot butter or margarine until golden. Put on to a heatproof dish, spread with apricot jam and quartered bananas. Sprinkle with brown sugar and heat under the grill (broiler).

Fruit Pancakes

Cooking time: 15 minutes
Serves: 2 (4 small pancakes or 2 large ones) plus batter or pancakes left for another dish (they could be filled with cooked vegetables, fish or chicken in a sauce)
To store: see below.

MENU
Cream of Cabbage Soup (*page 14*)
Grilled (broiled) Fish and Mashed Carrots
Fruit Pancakes

To freeze: pancakes freeze excellently; add a teaspoon oil to the batter before cooking. Wrap well and use within 2 months.

IMPERIAL	METRIC	AMERICAN
for the batter	*for the batter*	*for the batter*
4 oz. flour, preferably plain	100 g. flour, preferably plain	1 cup flour, preferably all-purpose
pinch salt	pinch salt	pinch salt
1 egg	1 egg	1 egg
½ pint milk *or* milk and water	¼ litre (3 dl.) milk *or* milk and water	1¼ cups milk *or* milk and water
for frying	*for frying*	*for frying*
oil (*see method*)	oil (*see method*)	oil (*see method*)
for the filling and topping	*for the filling and topping*	*for the filling and topping*
4–6 oz. raspberries, strawberries *or* other soft dessert fruit	100–150 g. raspberries, strawberries *or* other soft dessert fruit	4–6 oz. raspberries, strawberries *or* other soft dessert fruit
little sugar	little sugar	little sugar

Make the pancake batter: sieve the flour, salt, add the egg and enough milk, or milk and water, to make a thick batter. Beat hard until smooth then gradually beat in the rest of the liquid. You can store half the un-cooked batter in a screw-topped jar and use just half for this dish, or make all the pancakes and store half (see note below).
To cook the pancakes: heat about 1 teaspoon of oil in a small frying or omelette pan (enough to give a thin layer over the base of the pan), or, if using a larger pan, you will need 1½–2 teaspoons oil. Pour in sufficient batter to give a wafer-thin covering. Cook for 2 minutes or until golden brown on the bottom side and ready to turn. You can tell this quite easily, for the pancake moves freely in the pan. Turn over and cook on the second side, then lift from the pan and keep hot while you cook another pancake in the same way.
To keep hot: stand on a plate over a pan of boiling water, or put on a plate in a slow oven, do not cover.
   Crush the fruit with a little sugar, put on to each pancake, roll or fold. Top with more sugar and serve.

To vary
Fruit Pancakes de Luxe: make and fill the pancakes as above, keep warm.
For 2 servings: put the juice of 1 large orange with 1 tablespoon sugar into the frying pan. Stir until the sugar has dissolved, add 1 tablespoon brandy or a liqueur (curaçao, apricot or cherry brandy, etc.). Heat for 1 minute, put in the pancakes, reheat for 1–2 minutes.
   This is a delicious party dish. Make and fill all the pancakes you require, then heat in the syrup just before serving.

To store Batter or Pancakes

Batter: put in a screw-topped jar or covered container in the refrigerator. Whisk the mixture well before cooking.

Pancakes: cook as the recipe above. Separate each cooked pancake with a square of waxed or greaseproof paper. Wrap in foil, keep in the refrigerator for several days.

Lemon Syllabub

No cooking
Serves: 2
To store: in a cool place. Serve within 24 hours.

MENU
Gammon with Mustard and Orange Sauce (*page 29*)
New *or* Creamed Potatoes
Cauliflower *or* Broccoli
Lemon Syllabub

To freeze: while this can be frozen for a very limited time, it is better served freshly made.

IMPERIAL	METRIC	AMERICAN
¼ pint thick cream	⅛ litre (1½ dl.) thick cream	⅔ cup heavy cream
½ large *or* 1 small lemon	½ large *or* 1 small lemon	½ large *or* 1 small lemon
2 oz. castor sugar	50 g. castor sugar	¼ cup granulated sugar
4 tablespoons dry white wine	4 tablespoons dry white wine	5 tablespoons dry white wine

Whip the cream until it just holds its shape. Add the *finely* grated 'zest' of the lemon, the lemon juice and sugar, then gradually whisk in the wine. Spoon into two glasses and chill well before serving.

To vary
Orange Syllabub: use orange juice instead of lemon, but as orange has less flavour than lemon use the 'zest' of a whole orange.

Raspberry Syllabub: use 2–3 tablespoons mashed raspberries instead of lemon juice, etc.

Caramel Mousse

Cooking time: see method
Serves: up to 6
To store: for 24 hours only in the refrigerator; longer spoils the texture.

MENU
Grapefruit and Prawn Cocktail (*page 8*)
Taunton Chicken (*page 44*) with Green Salad, New Potatoes and Peas
Caramel Mousse—as recipe and Note
Cheese and Biscuits

Freezing tends to spoil the light texture.

IMPERIAL	METRIC	AMERICAN
a quarter of the Caramel sauce, *page 69*	a quarter of the Caramel sauce, *page 69*	a quarter of the Caramel sauce, *page 69*
½ oz. gelatine	15 g. gelatine	2 envelopes gelatin
¼ pint water	⅛ litre (1½ dl.) water	⅔ cup water
2 oz. sugar	50 g. sugar	¼ cup sugar
¼ pint thick cream	⅛ litre (1½ dl.) thick cream	⅔ cup whipping cream
¼ pint thin cream	⅛ litre (1½ dl.) thin cream	⅔ cup coffee cream
3 egg whites	3 egg whites	3 egg whites
to decorate	*to decorate*	*to decorate*
more thick cream	more thick cream	more whipping cream
1 oz. browned almonds	25 g. browned almonds	just under ¼ cup lightly toasted almonds

Make the Caramel sauce as the recipe on page 69, or use part of the ready-made sauce. Soften, then dissolve the gelatine in the hot water; add to the caramel with the sugar, then allow this to cool and begin to stiffen slightly. Fold in the lightly whipped creams–whip the thick cream first then fold in the thin cream and re-whip (the mixture should just hold its shape), then the stiffly whisked egg whites. Spoon into glasses or a serving dish and when firm decorate with more cream and nuts.

Note. A very super party dessert is made if you use the yolks to make a thick custard with 1 pint (6 dl.–2½ cups) milk and 1 oz. (25 g.–3 tablespoons) sugar and you put this into the bottom of about six glasses or a large bowl and allow it to cool, then spoon the mousse over the top. Remember to simmer the egg yolks, milk and sugar *very slowly* to make the custard.

Orange and Sultana Syllabub

See colour picture, page 63

No cooking
Serves: 2
To store: in the refrigerator for a day.

MENU
(for a special occasion)
Smoked Salmon
Steak Diane (*page 26*)
New Potatoes and Peas
Orange and Sultana Syllabub

IMPERIAL	METRIC	AMERICAN
1 large egg white	1 large egg white	1 large egg white
1 oz. castor sugar	25 g. castor sugar	$\frac{1}{4}$ cup granulated sugar
2 oranges	2 oranges	2 oranges
3 tablespoons white wine	3 tablespoons white wine	4 tablespoons white wine
$\frac{1}{4}$ pint thick cream	$\frac{1}{8}$ litre ($1\frac{1}{2}$ dl.) thick cream	$\frac{2}{3}$ cup heavy cream
few sultanas	few sultanas	few sultanas

Whisk the egg white until it is very stiff, then gradually whisk in all the sugar. Halve one orange and squeeze out all the juice, then peel the remaining $1\frac{1}{2}$ oranges and take out the pulp, cut this into neat pieces. Gradually whisk the orange juice and white wine into the stiffly beaten egg white. Whip the cream until it stands up in peaks. Fold this into the egg white mixture, together with the orange pulp and sultanas. Spoon into 2 individual glasses, chill for a short time then serve.

Note. If you prepare this some time before it is required it is a good idea to keep it in a basin, then stir gently just before spooning into the glasses.
Well drained canned mandarin oranges could be used in this recipe.

Caramel Custard

Cooking time: 2–2$\frac{1}{2}$ hours
Serves: 4–5
To store: in a cool place for up to 2 days.

MENU
This is an ideal dessert to make when you have the oven set very cool. It can be made before you require to serve it.

Do *not freeze* unless you use *half* milk and *half* cream in the custard.

IMPERIAL	METRIC	AMERICAN
1 pint milk (*or* use $\frac{3}{4}$ pint milk and $\frac{1}{4}$ pint thin cream)	$\frac{1}{2}$ litre (6 dl.) milk (*or* use $\frac{3}{8}$ litre (4$\frac{1}{2}$ dl.) milk and $\frac{1}{8}$ litre (1$\frac{1}{2}$ dl.) thin cream)	2$\frac{1}{2}$ cups milk (*or* use 2 cups milk and $\frac{1}{2}$ cup coffee cream)
either strip lemon rind *or* few drops vanilla essence (*optional*)	either strip lemon rind *or* few drops vanilla essence (*optional*)	either strip lemon rind *or* few drops vanilla extract (*optional*)
3 large eggs *or* 4 egg yolks	3 large eggs *or* 4 egg yolks	3 large eggs *or* 4 egg yolks
1 *or* 2 teaspoons sugar*	1 *or* 2 teaspoons sugar*	1 *or* 2 teaspoons sugar*
a quarter *or* half* of the Caramel sauce, *page 69*	a quarter *or* half* of the Caramel sauce, *page 69*	a quarter *or* half* of the Caramel sauce, *page 69*

* depending upon how much you like.

You need a tin, without a loose base, or a dish with a capacity of 2 pints (1 litre–5 cups) and about 3 inches (8 cm.) in depth. Heat the milk, or milk and cream, with the lemon rind or essence. Beat the eggs, or egg yolks, and the sugar, then add the hot milk. Pour the cold Caramel sauce into the tin or dish, strain the custard carefully into this. Cover the top with buttered foil or paper.

Either cook in a steamer over very hot but *NOT* boiling water, or cook in a tin of water in the oven. Allow approximately 2–2$\frac{1}{2}$ hours (depending upon the depth of mixture). The oven temperature should be very cool, 300°F (150°C), Gas Mark 2. The custard is sufficiently set when it feels firm and a small knife inserted in the centre comes out quite 'clean' with no un-set custard. Turn the custard out on to a large serving dish when it is cool. If you find some of the Caramel sauce still remains in the cooking utensil, warm this very slightly then spoon carefully over the custard.

Chocolate Mousse

Cooking time: few minutes
Serves: 2
To store: keep for up to 12 hours in the refrigerator. If kept longer the mixture becomes too firm.

MENU
Fish Pâté (*page 10*)
Veal Marengo (*page 36*) with Peas and Noodles
Chocolate Mousse

To freeze: freeze, cover and store for 3–4 weeks only. Too long freezing tends to spoil the light texture.

IMPERIAL	METRIC	AMERICAN
2 oz. plain chocolate	50 g. plain chocolate	2 oz. unsweetened chocolate
1 egg	1 egg	1 egg
3 tablespoons thick cream	3 tablespoons thick cream	scant ¼ cup heavy cream

Break the chocolate into pieces. Separate the egg and put the yolk into a basin with the chocolate. Beat over a pan of hot water until smooth and thick. Allow to cool, but not set again, then fold in the whipped cream and the stiffly whisked egg white. Spoon into two glasses and serve with plain biscuits if you want to make a more substantial dessert.

Strawberry Roll Chantilly

See colour picture, page 59

No cooking
Serves: 2
To store: this is at its best if stored for 1–2 hours before serving.

MENU
Trout with Almonds (*page 20*)
New Potatoes and Cauliflower
Strawberry Roll Chantilly
Cheese and Biscuits

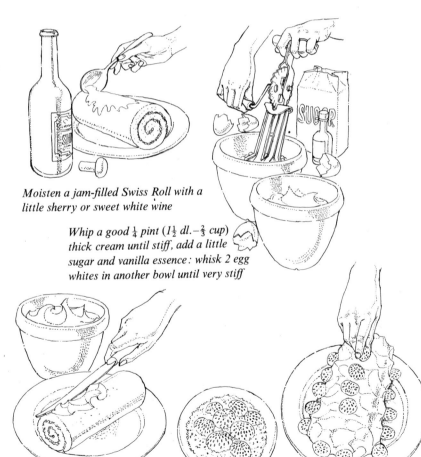

Moisten a jam-filled Swiss Roll with a little sherry or sweet white wine

Whip a good ¼ pint (1½ dl.–⅔ cup) thick cream until stiff, add a little sugar and vanilla essence: whisk 2 egg whites in another bowl until very stiff

Fold the sweetened cream into the stiffly whisked egg white: spread over the Swiss Roll, giving a 'swirling' effect

Decorate and serve with fresh strawberries, dusted with a little sugar, see picture, page 59

Budget Desserts

The following recipes are all inexpensive to make, *and* very good to eat.

Caramelled Rice

Cooking time: 40 minutes
Serves: 2
To store: in a cool place for 1–2 days.

MENU
Melon
Tongue in Port Wine Sauce (*page 42*)
Spinach
New *or* Sauté Potatoes
Caramelled Rice

To freeze: not satisfactory.

IMPERIAL	METRIC	AMERICAN
a quarter of the Caramel sauce, *page 69*	a quarter of the Caramel sauce, *page 69*	a quarter of the Caramel sauce, *page 69*
½ pint milk	¼ litre (3 dl.) milk	1½ cups milk
1 oz. round (Carolina) rice	25 g. round (Carolina) rice	2 tablespoons short grain (Carolina) rice
1 oz. brown sugar	25 g. brown sugar	2 tablespoons brown sugar
1 tablespoon blanched flaked almonds (*optional*)	1 tablespoon blanched flaked almonds (*optional*)	1 tablespoon blanched flaked almonds (*optional*)

Put the Caramel sauce, milk and rice into a basin or the top of a double saucepan over a pan of boiling water. Cook steadily for about 35 minutes, until the rice is tender. Spoon into a heatproof dish, top with sugar and almonds and brown under the grill (broiler). Serve hot or cold with cream.

To vary
Add a few sultanas, raisins or other dried fruit to the rice mixture, or flavour this with grated orange and lemon rind and omit the Caramel sauce. In this case sweeten the milk and rice.

Blackcurrant Soufflé

Cooking time: 15 minutes
Serves: 2
Eat as soon as baked.

MENU
Cheese and Beef Bake (*page 42*)
Blackcurrant Soufflé

Do *not* freeze.

IMPERIAL	METRIC	AMERICAN
1 oz. cornflour	25 g. cornflour	¼ cup cornstarch
½ pint milk	¼ litre (3 dl.) milk	1¼ cups milk
2 oz. sugar	50 g. sugar	¼ cup sugar
2 eggs	2 eggs	2 eggs
2–3 tablespoons blackcurrant syrup	2–3 tablespoons blackcurrant syrup	3–4 tablespoons blackcurrant syrup

Blend the cornflour with the milk. Pour into a saucepan and bring to the boil, stirring well as the mixture thickens. Add the sugar. Remove from the heat and whisk in the egg yolks and blackcurrant syrup. Fold in the stiffly whisked egg whites. Spoon into a greased soufflé dish and bake in the centre of a hot oven, 425–450°F (220–230°C), Gas Mark 6–7, until firm.
Rhubarb Soufflé: blend ½ pint thick rhubarb purée (sweetened) with 1 oz. sugar and yolks of 2 eggs. Fold in stiffly whisked egg whites. Spoon into greased soufflé dish and bake as above.

Raisin Fritters

Cooking time: 8 minutes
Serves: 2–3
Eat as soon as possible after they are cooked, although the batter may be made ahead and stored in the refrigerator.

MENU
Clear Onion Soup (*page 12*)
Savoury Cheese Balls (*page 56*) and Salad
Raisin Fritters

Do *not* freeze.

IMPERIAL	METRIC	AMERICAN
3 oz. seedless raisins	75 g. seedless raisins	½ cup seedless raisins
1 orange	1 orange	1 orange
milk (*see method*)	milk (*see method*)	milk (*see method*)
3 oz. self-raising flour*	75 g. self-raising flour*	¾ cup self-rising flour*
pinch salt	pinch salt	pinch salt
1 egg	1 egg	1 egg
for frying	*for frying*	*for frying*
1½ oz. fat	40 g. fat	3 tablespoons shortening
for the topping	*for the topping*	*for the topping*
little marmalade	little marmalade	little marmalade

* or use plain (all-purpose) flour and ¾ teaspoon baking powder (double acting).

Put the raisins into a basin. Add the grated orange rind (use the top 'zest' only). Squeeze the juice from the orange, measure this and add enough milk to give just ¼ pint (1½ dl.–⅔ cup); pour on to the raisins. Leave for 15 minutes, or longer if more convenient. Add the flour, sieved with the salt or salt and baking powder. Beat well to blend, then add the egg and beat again. Heat the fat in a frying pan. Drop in spoonfuls of the mixture and fry steadily for 2 minutes. Turn and cook for the same time on the second side. Lower the heat and cook for a further 3–4 minutes. Drain the fritters on absorbent paper. Put on to the serving dish, top with marmalade and serve.

To vary
Raisin and Apple Fritters: use 1 tablespoon less milk and add 1 peeled and grated apple to the batter mixture before cooking.

Summer Pudding

No cooking
Serves: 2–3
To store: this must be kept for at least 12 hours, and is nicer after longer storage. Keep in a cool place.

MENU
An ideal dessert to follow most main dishes.

To freeze: this freezes excellently. It can be stored for several months.

IMPERIAL	METRIC	AMERICAN
4–6 slices bread (*see method*)	4–6 slices bread (*see method*)	4–6 slices bread (*see method*)
½–¾ pint cooked sweetened fruit plus a little of the liquid from cooking	¼–⅜ litre (3–4½ dl.) cooked sweetened fruit plus a little of the liquid from cooking	1¼–2 cups cooked sweetened fruit plus a little of the liquid from cooking

You need enough bread to cover the bottom, sides and top of a small basin. Remove the crusts, put some of the bread at the bottom and the sides of the basin. Make sure it 'fits' neatly. Put in the fruit, cover with the rest of the bread. Put a piece of greaseproof paper or foil over the top, then a small weight. Leave for at least 12 hours, turn out, serve with cream, etc.

To vary
This is called Summer pudding, for the most usual fruits to put in are raspberries, loganberries, redcurrants, etc., or a mixture of these, but this pudding can be made throughout the year, varying the fruits according to the season.

Use slices of firm Madeira cake instead of bread.

Cooking for Two and 'A Bit'

When the time arrives that the family of two becomes two plus a child, there is the job of providing a meal for this small creature after he or she stops depending upon milk as the basic food. With a little thought and care it is possible to use some of the family menu to provide a good meal for the baby. Even very small children are given sieved vegetables, so if you cook an additional amount the night before, sieve or emulsify this and put it into a sealed container in your refrigerator *immediately* it is prepared, this may be warmed through gently for the baby. Spinach will lose a little of its vitamin, but so little that it is not a real problem. If you are cooking meat such as beef in the form of a steak, cut off a very small amount *after* it is cooked, chop, then sieve or emulsify or mince this and heat as required with a little milk or *pure* stock, avoiding any greasy gravy or sauce.

It may, however, be more practical to prepare the baby's meal, etc., the other way round, i.e. prepare a certain amount of your main meal midday, even if you and your husband are not having this until the evening, take out the amount required for the baby when it is freshly cooked and reheat gently for yourselves. There will still be a certain amount of last minute preparations, but with a little planning and consideration you can avoid an excessive amount of cooking to provide one or two tablespoons only of a certain food for a baby. *Do remember to:*

1 Be very careful about all storage containers; sterilise them with boiling water each time after use.

2 Be very careful that you do not store foods too long, even in the refrigerator. You can freeze tiny portions of baby food if you wish, but the moment they are thawed out you must use them quickly, and I would throw away any left over.

3 Do not give a baby highly spiced foods, follow the recommendations of your doctor or clinic.

Cooking for the Older Citizen

As one gets older you may find that your appetite decreases and there are certain foods that you can no longer eat with pleasure. Highly spiced foods, cooked cheese, etc., may give you indigestion. On the other hand, you may well find you are one of the lucky people who can 'eat everything', in which case your menus need not change. There are, however, certain points to remember:

Older people, just like young growing children, must have adequate protein, so do allocate a good percentage of your housekeeping money to the protein foods, meat, tripe, liver, eggs, fish, cheese, *milk,* and the protein vegetables, peas and beans, etc.

Calcium is as important when you are older as when you are growing. Older bones become brittle and break all too easily and an adequate supply of calcium is of great assistance in keeping the bones healthy. Cheese provides this, so use it as often as possible; if you cannot digest it when cooked, sprinkle on to soups, etc. Cream or cottage cheese are very easy to digest.

Vitamin C, in freshly cooked green vegetables, citrus fruits and some soft fruits such as strawberries, etc., is all important too. If you find green vegetables and fruit difficult to digest, chop the vegetables finely to make a purée, or squeeze out the fruit juice.

The recipes that follow are suitable for all the family, but they use valuable and reasonably inexpensive foods in a way that makes them equally suitable for an older person or a child.

Creamed Tripe

Cooking time: 55 minutes
Serves: 2
To store: for 2 or 3 days in the refrigerator. Cook enough for 2 meals, use some and reheat the rest, then add a little grated cheese or a beaten egg, heat gently, do not boil, just before serving.

This is one of the most economical, as well as easily digested meats.

Allow $\frac{3}{4}$–1 lb. (nearly $\frac{1}{2}$ kilo) tripe for two people. Cut this into neat fingers. Put into cold water, bring the water to the boil, throw this away (this blanches the tripe). Put the tripe and 1–2 sliced onions into milk, or milk and water, to cover. Season well. Simmer steadily for about 45 minutes or until tender. Thicken the milk, or milk and water, by blending 2 teaspoons cornflour (cornstarch) with a little cold milk. Stir into the liquid and cook steadily for several minutes. Add a small knob of margarine or butter.

To vary
Cook the tripe in stock, rather than milk, for a more savoury flavour.

Semolina Soufflé

Cooking time: 5 minutes
Serves: 2
Serve as soon as cooked.

MENU
Semolina Soufflé, thin Bread and Butter
Cooked Fruit

Do *not freeze*.

IMPERIAL	METRIC	AMERICAN
$\frac{1}{2}$ pint milk	$\frac{1}{4}$ litre (3 dl.) milk	$1\frac{1}{4}$ cups milk
1 small onion	1 small onion	1 small onion
2 teaspoons chopped parsley	2 teaspoons chopped parsley	2 teaspoons chopped parsley
seasoning	seasoning	seasoning
3 oz. semolina	75 g. semolina	$\frac{1}{2}$ cup semolina
2 oz. grated Cheddar cheese	50 g. grated Cheddar cheese	$\frac{1}{2}$ cup grated Cheddar cheese
2 eggs	2 eggs	2 eggs

This is an easy and economical savoury dish.

Bring the milk to the boil, add the chopped onion, parsley and seasoning. Whisk in the semolina gradually, then lower the heat and cook gently for about 10 minutes until a thick mixture. Add the cheese and eggs, mix well, spoon into a 5–6-inch (13–15-cm.) soufflé or ovenproof dish. Bake for 25 minutes in the centre of a moderate oven, 350–375°F (180–190°C), Gas Mark 4–5. Serve at once.

Liver Soufflé

Cooking time: 25 minutes
Serves: 2–3
This should be served as soon as cooked.

MENU
Irish Milk Soup (*page 14*)
Liver Soufflé with Jacket *or* Creamed Potatoes, sieved *or* chopped Spinach
Fresh Fruit

Do *not freeze*.

IMPERIAL	METRIC	AMERICAN
4 oz. cooked liver (*see page 46*)	100 g. cooked liver (*see page 46*)	4 oz. cooked liver (*see page 46*)
$\frac{1}{4}$ pint milk	$\frac{1}{8}$ litre ($1\frac{1}{2}$ dl.) milk	$\frac{2}{3}$ cup milk
2 tablespoons soft breadcrumbs	2 tablespoons soft breadcrumbs	2–3 tablespoons soft bread crumbs
$\frac{1}{2}$ oz. butter	15 g. butter	1 tablespoon butter
seasoning	seasoning	seasoning
2 eggs	2 eggs	2 eggs
1 egg white	1 egg white	1 egg white

Mince or chop the liver very finely. Put the milk and breadcrumbs into a fairly large saucepan, heat gently, add the liver, butter and seasoning; stir fairly constantly so you help to produce a reasonably smooth purée. Separate the eggs, beat the yolks into the mixture. Whisk the egg whites stiffly, fold into the liver mixture; then spoon the mixture into a greased 5–6-inch (13–15-cm.) soufflé or ovenproof dish. Bake for about 20 minutes in the centre of a moderate to moderately hot oven, 375–400°F (190–200°C), Gas Mark 5–6.

To vary
Use cooked chicken, ham or tongue in place of liver.

Fruit Condé

No cooking
Serves: 2
To store: do not open can until ready to prepare, then store in a cool place for 1 day.

Do *not freeze.*

IMPERIAL	METRIC	AMERICAN
small can creamed rice	small can creamed rice	small can creamed rice
little cooked, fresh *or* canned fruit	little cooked, fresh *or* canned fruit	little cooked, fresh *or* canned fruit
1–2 tablespoons redcurrant jelly	1–2 tablespoons redcurrant jelly	1–3 tablespoons redcurrant jelly

Open the can of creamed rice and pour this into a serving dish. Arrange the well drained fruit on top. Put the jelly with about 1 tablespoon of the fruit juice (or use fresh fruit juice) in a small pan, heat gently for a few minutes, cool slightly, then spread over the fruit.

Lemon Pudding

Cooking time: see method
Serves: 2 or even 3
To store: can be prepared and kept for a day before cooking, but is better cooked and eaten at once.

MENU
Pork Casserole (*page 36*) with Apple Sauce (*page 48*)
Brussels Sprouts
Lemon Pudding

To freeze: freezes well, use within about 2–3 months.

IMPERIAL	METRIC	AMERICAN
2 oz. margarine (soft type)	50 g. margarine (soft type)	¼ cup margarine (soft type)
2 oz. castor sugar	50 g. castor sugar	¼ cup granulated sugar
1 egg	1 egg	1 egg
2 oz. self-raising flour*	50 g. self-raising flour*	½ cup self-rising flour*
little lemon curd	little lemon curd	little lemon curd
½ lemon	½ lemon	½ lemon

* or use plain (all-purpose) flour and 1 teaspoon baking powder (double acting).

Put the margarine, sugar, egg and sieved flour, or flour and baking powder, into a basin and stir for about 2 minutes until blended. Put lemon curd at the bottom of a small pie dish or basin. Add the mixture. Either bake for approximately 35 minutes in the centre of a very moderate oven, 350–375°F (180–190°C), Gas Mark 4–5, or steam for 45 minutes. When the pudding comes from the oven, or is turned out, squeeze the lemon juice over it before serving.

Savoury Flan

No cooking
Serves: 2 as a main dish, 4 as a snack
To store: in a cool place for several days.

This is excellent for supper, or part of a buffet.

IMPERIAL	METRIC	AMERICAN
2 oz. butter *or* margarine	50 g. butter *or* margarine	¼ cup butter *or* margarine
seasoning	seasoning	seasoning
flavouring (*see method*)	flavouring (*see method*)	flavoring (*see method*)
4 oz. really crisp biscuits cheese-flavoured *or* plain	100 g. really crisp biscuits cheese-flavoured *or* plain	4 oz. really crisp crackers cheese-flavored *or* plain

Cream the butter or margarine with seasoning and flavouring. This can be a pinch of curry powder, celery salt, cayenne pepper or 1–2 tablespoons finely crumbled or grated cheese (any type of cheese can be used in this recipe). Crush the biscuits to form fine crumbs. Work into the creamed butter or margarine. Form into a 5–6-inch (13–15-cm.) flan shape. Chill, then fill as the pastry flan on page 58.

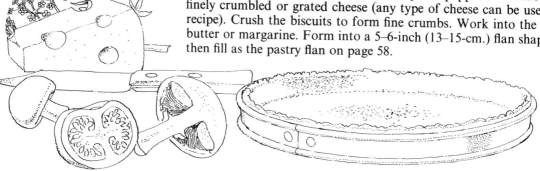

Index